No-Sew
SPECIAL EFFECTS

OTHER BOOKS AVAILABLE FROM CHILTON Robbie Fanning, Series Editor

No-Sew

SPECIAL EFFECTS

DONNA ALBERT

Chilton
BOOK COMPANY
RADNOR, PENNSYLVANIA

Copyright © 1996 by Donna Albert

All Rights Reserved
Published in Radnor, Pennsylvania 19089, by Chilton Book Company

Illustrations by Donna Albert and Sharon Tschudy, Trump Tschudy Design, Lancaster, Pennsylvania
Photographs by Jonathan Charles and Paul Jacobs, Charles Studio, Lancaster, Pennsylvania
Book design by Anthony Jacobson

Additional copies of this book may be ordered from any bookstore, or directly through Chilton Book Company (1-800-274-7066).

Manufactured in the United States of America

Library of Congress Cataloging-in-Publication Data
Albert, Donna.
    No-sew special effects / Donna Albert.
        p.   cm.
    Includes index.
    ISBN 0-8019-8718-0 (pbk)
    1. Textile crafts.   2. Fancy work.   3. House furnishings.
    I. Title.
TT699.A44   1996
746.9—dc20   96-17852
                                                        CIP

1 2 3 4 5 6 7 8 9 0   6 7 8 9 0 1 2 3 4 5

CONTENTS

CHAPTER 1:
GETTING STARTED   1

Discover expert tips on developing design ideas, selecting fabrics and materials, and creating unique, innovative projects with no-sew appliqué.

CHAPTER 2:
NO-SEW APPLIQUÉ   7

Learn the basic techniques essential to creating great no-sew appliqué every time, plus explore a wealth of easy, innovative variations.

Techniques

Projects

CHAPTER 3:
FABRIC MANIPULATION   23

Discover a wealth of simple, fascinating techniques for changing the "look" of any fabric.

Techniques

Projects

CHAPTER 4:
EMBELLISHMENTS   55

Learn how to decorate fabric surfaces with everything from ribbons and braids to buttons, beads, laces, and linens to create just the look you want.

Techniques

Projects

ACKNOWLEDGMENTS

With great appreciation, I want to thank the following people for all their help with this book:

First, my husband Chuck, for all his encouragement, support, and patience, as well as computer expertise, domestic skills, and overall endurance.

My mother and father, Mildred and Leon Wenrich, for teaching me the joy of working with my hands, and for the hours spent in the studio with me.

Mariann Lehmann and Cheryl Gross, two very special friends who helped me tremendously.

Esther Snyder and family, for all the quilting and the friendship.

Sharon Tschudy from Trump Tschudy Design, for hour after hour of her time drawing, and for her patience changing illustrations.

Jonathan Charles and Paul Jacobs from Charles Studio, for their skill and expertise in photography.

All the companies who generously provided products for me to experiment with in creating the designs in this book.

Susan Keller, Mary Green, and Jeff Day at Chilton for their help in getting my book published, as well as Anthony Jacobson for his stunning design. And a very special thank you to Barbara Ellis and Lynn McGowan for helping me organize my ideas and translate them into words and images.

INTRODUCTION

Welcome to No-Sew Special Effects

These days, finding time for creative expression seems an insurmountable task. Every day, we all seem to have less and less time for sewing, appliqué, quilting, and other crafts. *No-Sew Special Effects* is designed to come to the rescue of time-pressed crafters everywhere. Whether you want quick results, don't know how to sew at all, or are just plain impatient, you'll find that the techniques in this book will open doors for you. They are designed to excite and inspire sewers and non-sewers alike—from beginners to advanced fabric artists—and can be adapted to quilts, clothing, and home decorating items. Some projects are totally no-sew, including the construction. Others feature no-sew techniques but are sewn together with simple straight-line sewing. Most can be adapted either way.

My basic premise in writing this book can be summed up in an old Chinese saying, "Tell me and I forget. Show me and I remember. Involve me and I understand." Hands-on education is the best teacher. For this reason, each chapter includes a wealth of information on specific techniques, variations you can try, and projects you can make.

All the chapters are divided into two parts. In the first part, you will find basic information on different techniques, as well as loads of ideas to get you started experimenting with your own variations. "Tips for Success" pointers will help ensure professional results every time. The second part of each chapter is devoted to step-by-step projects you can use to experiment with the techniques. When you look at the projects, I hope you will view them in light of your own interests and look for ways to adapt them to make them truly yours. My goal is to inspire new thoughts, to encourage you to work with your hands, and to equip you with the confidence and skills to experiment with these new ideas, products, and techniques. Enjoy!

CHAPTER 1

GETTING STARTED

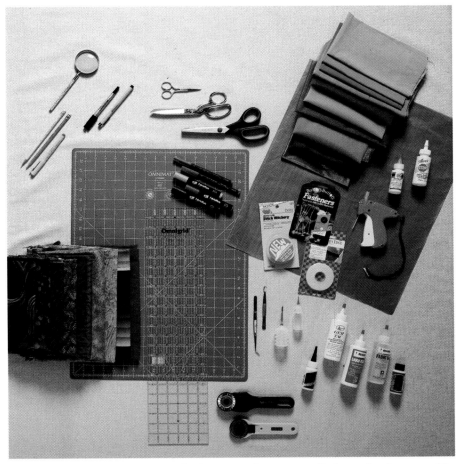

No-Sew Tools and Supplies. *To make designing and creating as effortless and as fun as possible, keep basic tools and supplies where they are handy to your work space.*

the opportunities for appliqué, transforming a time-consuming art into a quick and easy craft that nearly anyone can use to create a variety of attractive projects.

This book will help you explore many of these new tools and materials, and show you some of the ways they can be used. Below you will find a list of the types of materials and tools that should be on hand in any well-equipped workroom.

One essential "tool" you need is a pattern to follow. In this chapter, you will also find a basic guide to designing projects. I describe four basic steps—focus, format, fabric, and finishing—to help you understand the design process and motivate you to experiment and develop a style of your own. While this book provides you with a host of projects to try, I hope you will put some of your tools and ideas to work creating your own designs.

MATERIALS AND TOOLS FOR NO-SEW TECHNIQUES

Most of the materials you will need for the projects presented in this book are inexpensive and easy to

Ｎew products and tools have forever changed the way quilters and crafters create projects. Although many crafters still practice traditional techniques like hand quilting or hand appliqué, products such as rotary cutters, gridded rulers, and cutting mats now make it possible to cut fabric quickly and accurately. Fusibles have revolutionized

obtain. In fact, you probably already have many of them.

For best results, always read and follow the manufacturer's directions for the specific product you are using. Experiment with different products to determine which ones you prefer. When you are trying a new technique, reread the general information provided at the beginning of the chapter, as well as the step-by-step instructions for the project.

When you are fusing fabric, cover your ironing board with a piece of muslin or scrap fabric. Use a press cloth and a nonstick sheet whenever possible. Sooner or later, you will fuse adhesive to your iron and ironing board cover—probably sooner *and* later! Use iron cleaner to remove any residue from your iron. To remove adhesive from your ironing board cover, lay a dryer fabric softener sheet on top of the area, and iron over it.

In addition to a flat, clean work surface, you will need the following basic tools and materials to create no-sew projects:

Rotary cutter. Have replacement blades and decorative blades on hand, as well as a cutting mat and rulers designed specifically for use with rotary cutters.

Scissors. Use separate ones for paper and fabric. Sharp embroidery scissors and pinking shears also come in handy.

Iron. Use a steam iron, ironing board, pressing cloth, and a nonstick (Teflon) sheet.

Tacking board or design wall. Cover a wall or sheet of insulation with flannel or Pellon Fleece so you can hang your work vertically and step back and look at it easily.

Reducing glass. This tool allows you to view the pattern from a distance. A photograph also serves the same purpose.

Light box. A light box has a clear or frosted piece of glass or Plexiglas with light behind it. It is useful for tracing, since you can see a pattern through fabric. You can also use a light box to reverse patterns. (Or hold them up to a window, if you prefer.)

Designing and enlarging equipment. You will need pencils, erasers, rulers, a compass, and tracing paper for reversing patterns and designing your own. If you don't have access to a copier or enlarger, you will also need graph paper and a large roll of brown paper.

Materials for patterns. Acetate, plastic-coated freezer paper, oaktag, or thin cardboard (such as poster board) are all useful for making stencils, templates, or patterns. Use masking or drafting tape for taping the tracing paper to the pattern.

Materials for no-sew appliqué. For no-sew appliqué, you will need paper-backed fusible web and web tapes, liquid adhesives, fabric glues, plastic squeeze bottles with metal tips, glue applicators, brushes, hot tape, liquid fray preventative, spring-type clothespins or spring clips, and an assortment of pins.

Tweezers. This is an extremely versatile tool, especially for positioning small embellishments, such as beads and sequins. Tweezers are also handy for rearranging or placing small pieces of fabric, ribbons, braids, and trims.

Foamcore board or corrugated cardboard. These materials are useful for weaving and other techniques.

Fusibles. There are many types of fusible adhesives, ranging from paper-backed fusible web or web tape to fusible interfacings. Each works with different fabrics (for example, sheers or denims) and has a different purpose, from lightweight to heavy-duty. Fusibles will create a permanent bond when the materials and techniques are properly matched. Instructions differ among the various products; cleaning directions vary as well. If the product you have chosen doesn't give you the desired results, try a different one. Fusibles are available on bolts or in prepackaged, precut quantities. Fusible web tape comes in various widths and thicknesses. Fusible web is available with or without paper backing. (If you choose fusible web without paper backing, be sure to use a Teflon pressing sheet to avoid fusing the adhesive to the iron.) Flexible clear vinyl is useful for waterproofing and outdoor use. Heat-fusible adhesives include Pellon Wonder Under Transfer Web, Therm 'O Web Heat 'N Bond, Dritz Stitch Witchery with Grid, Fine Fuse, Aleene's Fusible Web, Steam-a-Seam, Pellon Fusible Fleece, and Beacon's LiquiFuse. Fusible interfacings include HTC Cool Fuse and Fusiknit, and Whisper Weft.

Fabric glues and liquid adhesives. This category includes Beacon's FabriTac and GemTac, Jones Tones Plexi 400 Stretch Adhesive, and Aleene's OK-to-Wash-It. FabriTac is an excellent choice and works well for most projects. It has a very fast "grab," dries quickly, and dries clear. (It's washable, too!) Because FabriTac bonds quickly, you only need to hold items in place a few seconds. Many other glues take longer to set and don't have as strong a bond. (Of course, these may be more suitable if you don't *want* the glue to set quickly.) GemTac works well for attaching embellishments such as beads or buttons.

TRANSLATING IDEAS INTO REALITY

There really isn't a right or wrong way to create a design. Each person designs differently—Some people plan every step; others work spontaneously with fabric and scissors. Regardless of your style, however, designing is a skill that needs to be developed and practiced.

As you design your own pieces, remember that you really *can* learn from your mistakes. Rather than failures, view them as learning experiences that will help you design your next piece. If you are extremely frustrated with an idea, put it aside and come back to it later; chances are, you will have a new perspective when you return. Stay open-minded and flexible, and don't be afraid to improvise. After a while, you will realize that ideas and designs are flowing. If you challenge yourself, grow through the process, and are pleased with the results or are motivated to experiment further, then your piece is successful.

Step 1: Focus

Where do ideas come from? Anywhere! Start with what appeals to you or interests you. Look for ideas in your everyday life, such as events, visual recollections, and vivid impressions. Designs and patterns are everywhere. In architecture, you can find them in the pattern of windows in a city scape, on floor tiles, or in wallpaper patterns. In nature, look for ideas in the shape of a leaf or in a landscape. A particular piece of fabric may spark an idea. Photographs from books and magazines or a family album can be translated into a textile creation. Seeing other artists work in a gallery or museum can also lead to original ideas.

Keep a notebook, sketchbook, or photo file of rough ideas. Every time you have an idea, write it down, sketch it, or photograph it. Don't worry about how rough the sketch or idea is; the point is to get it down before it's forgotten or lost. Include notes on color and texture. This visual research is crucial to creating inspired designs.

From those rough ideas and sketches, focus on a particular pattern, theme, or idea, and work with it. Don't be discouraged if your initial results aren't suc-cessful; stay with your design long enough to see if it will work. Try taking an image or idea from one context and combining it with other images or elements to create something new. If you have several thoughts about one idea or theme, think about doing a "series" based on that particular idea. Series pieces allow discovery by progressively building new ideas from other ideas—for example, by answering a question in several different ways and finding new solutions.

Asking questions can also help this process. Ask yourself if you want to make a statement, learn a technique, make a memento, or create a utilitarian piece for a particular place in your home. Knowing the purpose of the project will help you stay focused.

Step 2: Format

The next step is to turn your ideas into a usable design. To do this, you need to select a rough sketch and then redraw and rework it until a design appeals to you. An easy way to re-work a design is to use tracing paper overlays on the original sketch. Use a new overlay to redraw and rework the design as often as necessary.

For a design to work, the individual shapes and elements must be simplified and abstracted, and then arranged to form a blueprint or pattern. Whether you are designing a fabric picture, a geometric pattern, a repeating design, or a medallion, break it down into simple shapes, eliminating unnecessary elements. Study the relationship between the shapes, colors, and patterns. If you have difficulty with this concept, try a black-and-white photocopy; eliminating color helps to simplify the shapes. Cut the photocopy up, move the pieces around, then rearrange them again.

To work with geometric designs and repeating patterns, you may want to consider using a computer. There is a wide variety of software on the market for creating designs.

Step 3: Fabric

Selecting fabric that is just the right color, texture, and print can be intimidating. But the choices you make will have a major impact on the success of your project. If you are uncomfortable with the idea of selecting colors, remember that you choose them when you get dressed every day or decide which sofa to buy. The best way to gain experience is to plunge in and make some choices. You will find that the more you work with color, the more confident you become.

When selecting or arranging fabric, keep in mind that you need to organize the colors and textures to translate the design. Different color palettes create a mood, express feelings, or cause an emotional response. Warm colors such as yellow, orange, and red are energetic; cool colors like blue, green, and purple are reserved. Contrast is important as well. The eye will move directly to the areas of greatest contrast in a piece—a tendency you can use to advantage, by controlling where viewers look first.

For a successful design, you need a range of values and a variety of textures, as well as special-effect fabrics, for example, lamé, organdy, and iridescent fabric. Value, or the lightness or darkness of a color, is critical to establishing a pattern and creating contrast. Try not to disregard certain colors just because you don't like them; instead, try a different value of that color. Often, when a particular fabric doesn't work in a design, the value is wrong, not the color. One way to determine if a fabric is in value is to fold and stack the selected fabrics for a particular project, then squint at them; if one stands out, it's probably not in value. You can also use a value filter, a red piece of plastic that removes the colors, reducing them to values.

When you are selecting fabric, consider both the visual and the surface texture. Visual texture is created by the surface design or print of the fabric. The scale, or size, of the design or motif will affect the visual texture, as will the contrast between the colors used: The more contrast, the more texture and drama. Surface texture is the actual feel of the fabric. Surface textures vary widely, from sheer to corduroy, velvet to satin, suede to burlap.

Your choice of fabrics will also depend on the function of a finished piece. For example, fabric for clothing or home decorating items should be both durable and washable. Proper preparation is important, too. For utilitarian pieces, such as clothing, always launder the fabrics beforehand. In fact, it's a good idea to wash and dry most fabrics you plan to use in a project—especially those you will be dyeing or painting—to preshrink them and remove any finishes. (If you will be using the project as a wall hang-ing or for display only, it is not always necessary to wash the fabrics first, depending on the techniques used to create it.) Check for color fastness by placing a piece of wet fabric on a paper towel or white cloth; if color transfers to the paper towel, the fabric will bleed and should be set by adding salt or vinegar to the rinse water.

After selecting the fabric, use a design wall or Graph-tac to place the fabrics next to one another so you can study the relationships. (Graph-tac is a double-sided adhesive graph paper that can be used to determine how a design will look on a small scale.) Work on a tacking board made from a sheet of homosote or insulation covered in flannel or fabric to tack into, or a flannel board, which can simply be a piece of foamcore board covered with batting or flannel to lay your work on.

Step 4: Finishing

To finish the design process, you need to create a full-size pattern, transfer it to fabric, and then assemble the design. First, take the formatted design and enlarge it to actual size using a photocopier, enlarger, or overhead projector. (For large projects, work in sections and tape them together.) Make a full-size drawing or master pattern on tracing paper and outline it with a black marker. Number the pattern pieces for use as templates or to indicate the order of assembly. (Assembling should be done in a logical progression. In some designs, the order isn't critical, but when assembling a landscape, for instance, it is preferable to begin with the background and work toward the foreground.) To make a template, trace the pattern pieces, numbering each one with the corresponding number from the full-size pattern. Cut them out and use them to trace around. Do *not* cut up the master pattern when making templates.

Next, transfer the pattern to the selected fabric. If you use a tracing paper overlay, place the overlay on top of the background fabric, then slip the appliqué pieces between the two, moving the pieces around until they are in place. Or place the fabric on top of the master pattern over a light box or at a window, and trace the pattern lightly onto the background.

Designing a Fabric Painting

Fabric paintings are quite intriguing and not all that difficult to design. Photographs are excellent design tools for creating them, because they provide a permanent reference for proportion, placement of light and dark, patterning, and color. It is important that you do not try to reproduce a photograph exactly. Instead, work to develop a design that translates the mood, flavor, and atmosphere of it. Observe what attracts you to the photograph; study the shapes, forms, and textures.

Below are the steps I followed to transform a photograph into the Nantucket Fabric Painting, a project presented in Chapter 6. Try using the same procedure with a photograph—or a painting or drawing—to create a design of your own.

Nantucket Lighthouse Photo. *To see how a photograph can be broken down into simple shapes, compare this photograph of the Nantucket lighthouse with the line drawing (Fig. 1-1) of the same scene. Then turn to page 92 to see the color photo of the finished fabric painting.*

Fig. 1-1. *Creating an effective fabric painting—or any design for that matter—involves simplifying and abstracting individual shapes and eliminating unnecessary elements. Compare this line drawing with the color photograph of the Nantucket Fabric Painting to see how this process works.*

1 Make a good-quality, high-contrast black-and-white photocopy of the photograph. You may want to enlarge the photocopy to at least 5″ × 7″ so the shapes are large enough to work with. Use several views as a reference.

2 Lay a piece of tracing paper over the photocopy; trace the shapes. Simplify the design by tracing the main elements and eliminating many of the details. Treat the photocopy like a pattern: Rework the shapes, simplifying them, until you have created

a satisfactory design. (You can add details and other elements after simplifying the shapes.) To establish perspective, draw objects the way they appear visually, rather than the way they actually are. For example, objects appear smaller and higher up the farther away they are; parallel lines appear to be closer together the farther away they are. Objects in the foreground are more distinct and vivid than those in the background.

3 Make a full-size pattern or master pattern using a photocopier or opaque projector. Outline it with a dark marker.

4 Make several photocopies of the line drawing for your design, and color them in to see how the various colors affect the design. Then use these as a guide to help you select the fabrics. Choose fabrics that represent the color and texture of the subject. Or consider using techniques like overdyeing or discharge dyeing to create your own fabrics. (See Chapter 6 for details.)

5 Plan the sequence of assembly, and determine which pieces will overlap. (Generally, it's a good idea to work from the background to the foreground.) If there are numerous pattern pieces in the design, number them according to their order of placement. (See Figures 6-2 through 6-6 to see how the *Nantucket Fabric Painting* was assembled.)

CHAPTER 2

NO-SEW APPLIQUÉ

Appliqué is a technique that offers great creative freedom. Traditionally, it is done by cutting out pieces of one fabric and carefully hand-sewing them onto another to create a pattern or a picture. But the invention of fusible adhesives has led to quick and easy no-sew methods for creating appliqué. In this chapter, you will find information on a variety of these exciting no-sew appliqué techniques, along with ideas to get your creative juices flowing and projects that allow you to practice the techniques.

BASIC NO-SEW APPLIQUÉ

Basic no-sew appliqué is a fast, easy technique that uses fusible adhesives to create appliqué. It is extremely flexible, and lends itself to creating imagery from various sources, including photographs, line drawings, and paintings. It also allows for developing patterns as a decorative element. It is not surprising, then, that most of the projects in this book use this technique.

Whimsical Cat and Dog Banners. *These simple banners are made with basic no-sew appliqué and are a good way to try out this extremely versatile technique. Directions for these projects begin on page 16.*

No-Sew How-To

The following are complete step-by-step directions for this all-important technique. To ensure great results every time, review these steps before you begin any of the projects in this book.

1 **Wash the fabric.** Fusible adhesives generally adhere better to fabric that has been washed to remove any sizing. Always prewash fabric for quilts or other projects that will be routinely washed. Fabric that you intend to paint or dye must also be washed, as well as dried. However, you don't have to wash fabrics for wall hangings or other items that won't be laundered.

2 **Make a reverse master pattern.** When you are working with paper-backed fusibles, the final image will be reversed from the pattern unless you reverse it first. Of course, this doesn't matter if you are working with a symmetrical design, such as the one for the *Bird Nest Block* in Chapter 4. However, for any asymmetrical design, including lettering, you'll need to make a reverse master pattern if you want your finished project to look just like the original pattern. To do this, turn the pattern over and

outline it with a dark marker. Then trace the reversed pattern onto the paper side of the fusible web. Don't try to trace the entire pattern all at once; instead, trace each shape individually, allowing space around each one. A light box makes tracing easier; you can also hold the pattern up against a window. Use a tracing paper overlay if you don't want to mark on the pattern itself.

3 **Mark the pattern pieces.** Mark your pattern pieces with a number or other code to help you keep track of how they are supposed to be placed on the background fabric. I generally number the pieces in the order that they are fused in place. For example, a vase would be fused onto the background before the flowers and the leaves. The vase would be numbered "1," and flowers or leaves in the background would have lower numbers than those in the foreground.

4 **Cut out the traced fusible pieces.** Cut out the appliqué shapes from the fusible web, allowing at least 1/8″ to 1/4″ extra space beyond the pencil line (Fig. 2-1). Neatness doesn't count here—Just rough-cut around the pieces of fusible. With larger pieces, it's a good idea to trim out the interior of each shape to reduce bulk and prevent stiffness (Fig. 2-2).

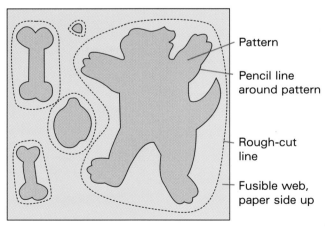

Fig. 2-1. Trace the appliqué shapes onto the paper side of the fusible adhesive, then rough-cut them from the fusible following the dotted line, as shown. Keep in mind that shapes are drawn in the reverse of the finished appliqués.

5 **Fuse the web pieces to the fabric.** Place your fabric wrong side up on an ironing board or other flat surface, then place the fusible web, paper

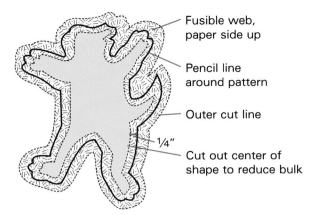

Fig. 2-2. To avoid stiffness in an appliqué, cut out the center of the fusible piece.

side up and rough side down, on top of it. Following the manufacturer's directions for the fusible you have selected, place an iron on the paper side of the fusible for the specified time. Lift the iron up and down (do *not* glide it back and forth) to bond the fusible to the fabric.

6 **Cut out the shapes.** Cut out each appliqué shape, following the pencil line drawn on the paper side of the fusible web. This produces pieces of fabric the same size as the original pattern, with fusible web on the wrong side.

7 **Remove the backing.** After the paper backing has cooled, remove it from each shape by bending a corner or edge toward the paper side. The paper should separate easily from the fabric. Be sure the paper is cool; if you remove it too soon, the glue may not be bonded to the fabric. Save the paper to use as a protective press cloth. (For complex designs, remove the paper as you position the shapes, to keep track of their order of placement.)

8 **Arrange and fuse.** Lay the pieces on the background fabric and rearrange them until you are satisfied with their placement. (When working with appliqué shapes that have a common meeting point, overlap the edges approximately 1/16″ to 1/8″ to prevent a gap between shapes.) Fuse the design in place following the manufacturer's directions for the fusible web you are using. Again, lift the iron up and down to press the pieces in place; moving it back and forth will cause the pieces to shift position, which can spoil your carefully planned arrangement.

Tips for Success

NO-SEW

♦ When using a fusible adhesive, always follow the manufacturer's directions, and test the product on a sample of the fabric you plan to use to see how well it bonds.

♦ Trace and cut the shapes carefully—It is worth taking your time.

♦ Wash the fabrics before fusing, to remove any sizing; otherwise, they may not bond sufficiently.

♦ Press the fabrics before fusing or wrinkles and marks will be bonded permanently.

♦ Do *not* overheat the fusible web. Overheating can cause the adhesive to melt through the fabric or not work properly. If little marks from the holes in the iron show, *gently* move the iron over them to smooth them out.

♦ Use a pressing cloth for fine or sheer fabric to prevent scorching.

♦ When fusing a large piece, start pressing in the middle and work outward.

♦ To protect the ironing board from the adhesive, work on a Teflon press sheet or a piece of scrap fabric. If any adhesive gets on the iron or the board, iron over a sheet of fabric softener to remove it.

♦ Thicker fabric requires more pressing. When bonding two fabrics (thicknesses) together, iron from the thinner side, and apply pressure.

♦ Fusible adhesives have no grain, so they can be cut and applied in any direction.

♦ Cut edges of fabric backed with fusible web can be exposed because they will not ravel.

♦ Thicker fusible webs add stiffness or body to appliqués.

DIMENSIONAL APPLIQUÉ

Dimensional appliqué does just what its name suggests: It adds a third dimension to appliqué. Layering

Vase with Lilies Wall Hanging. *Several types of dimensional appliqué are featured in this wall hanging to give the flowers a natural, three-dimensional effect. Directions for this project begin on page 17.*

pieces on top of one another is the most basic way to add dimension to a project. Padding or stuffing shapes adds even more dimension, creating a softly textural, low-relief effect. Knitted fabrics are especially suitable for stuffing or padding, since they stretch. The choice of padding depends on the desired effect. Oaktag, card stock, and cardboard all provide a hard, defined edge, while fusible fleece or batting creates a soft, fluffy, more pliable look. Layering felt or fleece produces an effect that is neither hard nor soft, but somewhere

Vase with Lilies Materials. *With careful cutting, the shells on one of the fabrics used to make this piece were transformed into lily petals*

in between the two. Cardboard can also be covered, then stuffed with fiberfill to soften it.

You can also add dimension by using reversible, or two-sided, fabric. For example, fuse fabric wrong sides together and cut a shape from it. Then attach the shape to a project on one side only with fabric glue. Let the rest of the shape project out from the project's surface to create a dimensional effect. This technique is especially effective when used to represent natural forms such as leaves, flowers, bird wings, or even figures.

Another option is to construct pliable, three-dimensional appliqué. For instance, you can sandwich screening, wire mesh, or even wire inside a reversible, or two-sided, appliqué shape to mold a form. (Keep in mind that the finer the wire, the more malleable it is. However, fine wire may not hold its shape as well as heavier-gauge wire.) A flexible armature or framework for soft sculptural forms also can be devised by wrapping strands of electrical wire with fabric and then applying it to a piece.

When creating dimensional appliqués, experiment with various fusible materials. The strength of the bond varies, depending on the type of product used. The paper-backed sheets of adhesive tend to work better than other fusibles for bonding padded and free-form appliqués. The *Vase with Lilies Wall Hanging* illustrates several ways you can add dimension to appliqué.

MOSAIC APPLIQUÉ

Traditional mosaic is an ancient art form that uses colored pebbles, pieces of glass, or small glazed tiles set in mortar to create a picture or decorative design. The frame for the *Vase with Lilies Wall Hanging* features a mosaic appliqué pattern. This useful technique is ideally suited to no-sew appliqué. Bits and pieces of fabric are arranged on a piece of background fabric to create a composition, and are then fused in place. Mosaic appliqué can have an impressionistic or pointillistic style, or you can simply combine irregular shapes that visually collide to form a rhythmic pattern. Another option is to draw a grid and arrange the pieces of fabric in a geometric pattern, much like the traditional mosaic used on cathedral floors. Use fabric color and texture to create forms and figures or to simply create a rhythmic design full of motion.

Design Ideas—Mosaic Appliqué

Mosaic appliqué is a terrific way to use up all those

Mosaic Appliqué Frame. *Mosaic appliqué, used to create the frame for the* Vase with Lilies Wall Hanging, *is a fascinating and fun technique that you can use to make all sorts of patterns and pictures. Directions for this project begin on page 19.*

Mosaic Appliqué Materials. *As you can see from the sampling of fabrics used to create this frame, mosaic appliqué is a great technique for using up bits of leftover fabric*

scraps of fabric you've been saving! Textured fabrics and old, torn scraps that are otherwise useless are ideal for this technique. In fact, a variety of textures and fabrics generally adds interest to this type of appliqué. In addition, consider making marbled or scrunch-dyed fabric to cut up. (See "Marbling" in Chapter 5 and "Scrunch Dyeing" in Chapter 6 for details on these techniques.)

Don't worry about cutting out your mosaic shapes perfectly; a variety of shapes and edges adds to the effect. Keep in mind that the smaller the mosaic shapes are, the more detailed the design can be.

BRODERIE PERSE

Broderie Perse, sometimes referred to as Persian embroidery, involves cutting motifs and shapes from one printed fabric and appliquéing them on another background. Cut-out motifs and shapes can be used separately, or they can be arranged into a picture. The fused shapes can then be enhanced by gluing trim around them. The *Petroglyph Duvet Cover and Pillow Shams* (shown right) feature this exciting technique.

Traditionally, Broderie Perse was considered an inexpensive imitation of embroidery. Oriental florals and chintz prints with birds, baskets, and flowers were used, and the images were sewn in place with fancy decorative stitches. Today, fusible adhesives make this an easy way to create unique appliqués. It's a great technique for both beginners and impatient crafters, since there is no need to reverse patterns or fuss with cutting templates. But Broderie Perse is also very rewarding for advanced quilters and crafters, because it offers a wealth of possibilities. For example, it can be used for everything from creating a border for a quilt to making a child's play mat.

Design Ideas—Broderie Perse

One of the best ways to get started with Broderie Perse is to let fabrics inspire your design. Instead of drawing your own pattern, search for fabrics that can be used as actual figures, motifs, and patterns. Look at the individual elements in the design—the flowers, cats, paisleys, geometric shapes, and so on—and experiment with ways to use them in a different context. Overlay the shapes to build a different picture or design.

Try using many different fabrics—from decorator to pictorial-style—with a variety of textures and colors. Combining several fabrics not only adds interest, it also provides balance. For example, motifs in fabrics are often printed in one direction only; using other fabrics with coordinating or similar motifs can help offset this imbalance.

STAINED GLASS APPLIQUÉ

Stained glass appliqué is dramatic looking and very easy to create with no-sew techniques. One way to make it is to cut out shapes of color, without seam allowances, and mount them on a foundation fabric. Then use dark, contrasting bias binding or ribbon to

USING BRODERIE PERSE

The *Petroglyph Duvet Cover and Pillow Shams* shown here give a contemporary look to a traditional technique—Broderie Perse. You don't need a pattern to create a design like this one: It was worked out directly on a purchased duvet cover and pillow shams. Squares of hand-stamped spiral fabric were combined with various motifs cut from one individual fabric that complemented the duvet cover. These were then fused in place in a random pattern on the top side of the pillow shams and duvet cover. Next, black-and-white checkerboard cotton ribbon was cut into squares and included in the pattern on the duvet. On the other side of the duvet cover as well as on the pillow shams, cotton ribbon was fused on to form a border, creating a reversible duvet.

The amount of fabric needed for this type of project varies according to the size of the motifs to be cut out, the number of motifs required for the design, and the dimensions of the object you are decorating. Try to estimate how much you will need, but always buy more fabric than you think you will need so you will have enough on hand.

With a large project like this one, it is best to work on a large, flat surface. If a large surface isn't available, work in sections. Always wash the fabrics before you start, and be sure to place padding underneath your work before fusing.

Art Nouveau Stained Glass Window. *An overlay of black fabric is used to create the illusion of a stained-glass window. This translucent hanging is especially effective if hung where light will shine through it. Directions for this project begin on page 20.*

Stained Glass Window Materials. *Gold threads in the red and green fabrics give the illusion of glittering glass. Flat black fabric gives the "leading" a solid feel.*

cover the raw edges of the cut-out shapes. The bias binding outlines the pieces of fabric and represents the leading in a traditional stained glass window. Use ribbon on geometric designs; use bias tape or binding for designs with curves, since it has elasticity and can be manipulated. Be careful not to stretch or distort the bias strips. (If you make your own bias tape, use cotton, which holds a crease well.) As you fuse the binding, hide as many ends as possible under another piece of bias tape so the design will be smooth. Cut the strips at an angle, if necessary, so they meet smoothly.

The other option for creating stained glass appliqué is to cut out the "leading" from one large piece of fabric, lay it on top of the design, then fuse it in place. This method, which I used to make the *Art Nouveau Stained Glass Window*, is especially useful when there are intersecting points and curves.

With either technique, the width of the leading needs to be appropriate to the design. (Leading that is too thick will overwhelm the colored "glass" insets, for example.) In addition, all of the leading must interconnect and lead to the outside edges; otherwise, the stained glass effect will be lost.

Design Ideas—Stained Glass Appliqué

Simple designs with bold shapes and rich colors are most effective for this technique; it's best to avoid small shapes or sharp curves. Stained glass appliqué is great for Celtic designs and church banners, and real stained glass windows are an obvious source for ideas.

This technique is ideal for pieces through which light shines, such as curtains, blinds, lampshades, or a fabric stained glass window like the one featured in this chapter. (Keep in mind that fabric will fade if left in a window for a long time, but don't be afraid to hang it there for special occasions or holidays.)

SHADOW APPLIQUÉ

Shadow appliqué uses sheer fabrics as overlays on top of brighter fabrics to create muted tones that suggest shadows. The basic technique involves placing a design or motif on a piece of background fabric and then completely covering it with a sheer fabric, such as organza, chiffon, georgette, net, tulle, or batiste. The motif is then outlined with a running or quilting stitch.

Shadow appliqué is effective for blending colors together, because the overlay adds the same tone to all the fabrics it covers, making them more harmo-

Pinwheel Window Curtain. *This elegant curtain is created with translucent and opaque fabrics using shadow appliqué. This technique is especially effective when light shines through the finished piece. Directions for the project begin on page 21.*

nious. The muted colors that are created lend a very soft, airy effect to a piece. (Pastel fabrics under a sheer overlay can have a delicate appearance, but intense colors provide richer results.) Since the overlay is sheer, it also adds very little bulk to a piece.

Shadow appliqué is ideal for projects through which light will filter, such as lampshades or window coverings like the *Pinwheel Window Curtain*. You can even use it to create a unique shower curtain.

SCHERENSCHNITTE APPLIQUÉ

Scherenschnitte, meaning "scissors cut," is a traditional technique for creating motifs and scenes by folding and cutting paper. The openwork creates a delicate design and gives an illusion of complexity even if the pattern is simple. This technique is especially useful for creating symmetrical patterns. The patterns can be simple and require very little time, or they can be extremely complex, involving meticulous work. All you need to design a pattern are a pencil, paper, and sharp scissors.

The *Christmas Tree Skirt* project illustrates some of the possibilities using this technique, which has a charming, folk art look. In fact, many countries—including Germany, Switzerland, Poland, Japan, and Mexico—have scherenschnitte traditions. (Another closely related technique is Hawaiian appliqué, which also involves folding and cutting patterns.) Common motifs include hearts, flowers, and animals. The popular fleur-de-lis patterns from the Baltimore Album Quilts can be created this way.

Traditionally, scherenschnitte is done in two colors, but you can combine more colors or even include printed fabrics. For best results, choose strongly contrasting colors to accentuate the design.

Making your own designs using this technique is easy, but keep the scale in mind when you make patterns. Also, practice the technique before you attempt very small or intricate cuts.

Tips for Success

CREATING AND CUTTING SCHERENSCHNITTE PATTERNS

- ♦ If you are making your own patterns, keep in mind that the folded part of the paper forms the center of the design when the paper is opened up. Also, remember that the entire design needs to be connected. Draw your design to indicate the portions that are going to be cut out; the portions that touch the folded edges are connecting points. (To make it easier to see your design clearly, you can lightly shade in the portions you want to cut away.) It's a good idea to work on paper, cut out the design, then use it as a pattern.

- ♦ Use scissors with small blades and sharp points. Surgical scissors, manicure scissors, small sewing scissors, and embroidery scissors all work fine.

- ♦ To make a smooth cut, start cutting with the portion of the blades closest to the apex; finish the cut without closing the blades completely. Be sure the blades are open before you pull the scissors away.

- ♦ Begin by making the smallest inside cuts first. To start the interior cuts, either pierce with the points of the scissors, or fold the piece in half and make a "V" cut large enough to start cutting. Cut from the pierced point out, toward the line. Then follow the line.

- ♦ As you cut, move your design rather than the scissors.

SCHERENSNITTE CHRISTMAS TREE SKIRT

Who hasn't cut out snowflakes or paper dolls from crisp sheets of white paper—or colored construction paper, for that matter? This *Christmas Tree Skirt* demonstrates how this simple technique can be used to create a family heirloom. It uses scherenschnitte (scissors cut) appliqué—in this case, simple shapes cut from double-folded and triple-folded cut-paper patterns—to make a charming scene. The design for the skirt is repeated in quarters.

Cut out a 28"-diameter circle from felt to make the skirt. The patterns for this project are all created from a piece of paper folded in half, with the design drawn on one side. This method results in a symmetrical design when the folded piece is opened up. If you are creating your own patterns, it may help to think of each design as one-half a design. You can also create some patterns by folding paper in quarters. Trace the designs onto fusible fleece and then cut them and fuse them into place.

Whimsical Cat and Dog Banners

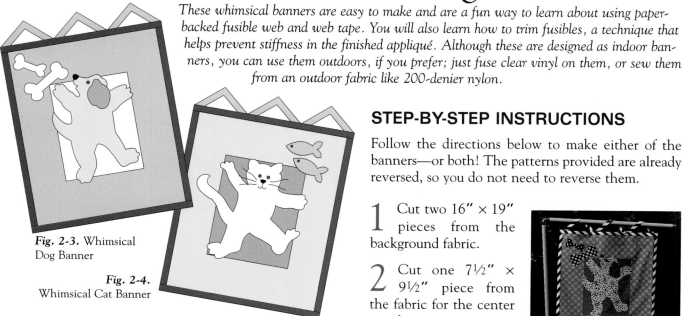

These whimsical banners are easy to make and are a fun way to learn about using paper-backed fusible web and web tape. You will also learn how to trim fusibles, a technique that helps prevent stiffness in the finished appliqué. Although these are designed as indoor banners, you can use them outdoors, if you prefer; just fuse clear vinyl on them, or sew them from an outdoor fabric like 200-denier nylon.

Fig. 2-3. Whimsical Dog Banner

Fig. 2-4. Whimsical Cat Banner

Finished Size. 15″ × 18″.
Technique. Basic no-sew appliqué.
Patterns. Pages 114–115.

FABRIC AND SUPPLIES

- ½ yd. background and backing fabric for *each* banner: blue check fabric for the Dog Banner; yellow check for the Cat Banner
- ¼ yd. fabric for central panel of *each* banner: cobalt blue for the Dog Banner; coral for the Cat Banner
- ⅓ yd. fabric for the central image: spotted fabric for the Dog Banner; striped fabric for the Cat Banner
- Miscellaneous scraps of fabric for bones and fish
- 5 yds. binding (and tabs): 2½ yds. for each banner
- ½ yd. paper-backed fusible web
- 7 yds. of ⅜″ paper-backed fusible web tape: 1 yd. for each banner and 2½ yds. for each binding
- Fabric glue
- Buttons or other embellishments for eyes
- ⅓ yd. decorative trim for cat's whiskers
- Optional: two 16″ × 19″ pieces fusible fleece or batting

STEP-BY-STEP INSTRUCTIONS

Follow the directions below to make either of the banners—or both! The patterns provided are already reversed, so you do not need to reverse them.

1 Cut two 16″ × 19″ pieces from the background fabric.

2 Cut one 7½″ × 9½″ piece from the fabric for the center panel.

3 Fuse ⅜″ paper-backed fusible web tape along each edge of the 7½″ × 9½″ piece of center panel fabric.

4 Remove the paper backing, and position the center panel on one of the 16″ × 19″ pieces of background fabric, following the pattern. Fuse it in place, following the directions under "No-Sew How-To" earlier in this chapter.

5 Trace the cat and fish or dog and bones on paper-backed fusible web. Cut out the traced shapes, then fuse them to the selected fabric. Cut out the shapes from the fabric, and fuse them in place on the background fabric, following the pattern.

6 Lay the backing fabric (the other 16″ x 19″ piece cut in Step 1), right side down, on a flat surface. Layer the batting and banner on top, matching the edges. Pin in place. Mark and trim the edges to measure 15″ × 18″.

7 Fuse or sew the binding on, then add the tabs. (See "Banner Binding" in Chapter 7 for detailed instructions on binding and adding tabs.)

Vase with Lilies Wall Hanging

This wall hanging uses a variety of techniques to create three-dimensional effects. Since many of the appliqué pieces are small, the project provides a great way to use scraps of fabric left over in your workbasket. The petals of the lilies are cut from a single piece of fabric with large fish and shell motifs. The vase has been cut from three pieces of transparent fabric to create a glasslike effect. Directions for making the Mosaic Appliqué Frame follow this project.

Finished Size. Center block: 10″ × 14″; 18″ × 22″, including the 4″ mosaic border.
Techniques. Dimensional appliqué, basic no-sew appliqué.
Pattern. Page 116.

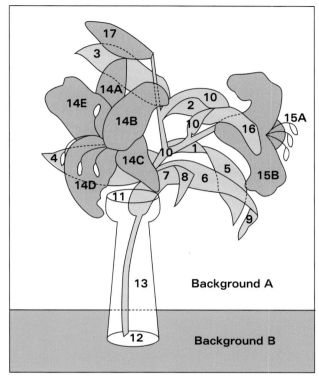

Fig. 2-5. Vase with Lilies Wall Hanging

FABRIC AND SUPPLIES

11½″ × 10½″ piece of light fabric for Background A

3½″ × 10½″ piece of dark fabric for Background B

⅛ yd. or scraps of light green fabric for leaves and stems

⅛ yd. or scraps of medium green fabric for leaves and stems

⅛ yd. or scraps of dark green fabric for leaves and stems

Fabric scraps for flowers

⅔ yd. fabric for backing

20″ × 24″ piece of batting, plus extra scraps of fusible fleece or batting for padding appliqué shapes

Scrap of transparent fabric for vase

Scraps of black fabric for stamens

⅔ yd. paper-backed fusible web

⅓ yd. of ⅜″ paper-backed fusible web tape

Paper- or fabric-wrapped florist's wire

Aluminum screening or mesh

Fabric glue

Fabric marker

MAKING THE BACKGROUND

1 Measure and cut an 11½″ × 10½″ piece of light fabric for Background A and a 3½″ × 10½″ piece of dark fabric for Background B.

2 Apply ⅜″ paper-backed fusible web tape along the top edge of Background B and fuse it to Background A.

CUTTING OUT THE SHAPES

1 Following the directions in "No-Sew How-To" earlier in this chapter, cut out all of the appliqué shapes from paper-backed fusible web. Be sure to reverse the pattern before tracing the shapes. Also, when you rough-cut the traced fusible pieces, remember to allow ¼″ or so from the traced pattern line. Be sure to mark the numbers on the pattern pieces as you cut them out.

2 Using the guide below, fuse the traced pattern pieces onto the wrong side of the fabrics listed. (If you choose an opaque fabric for the vase, eliminate pattern piece 12.)

Light green leaf fabric: 1, 2, 3, 4, and 6.
Medium green leaf fabric: 5, 8, 9, 16, and 17.
Dark green leaf fabric: 7 and 10.
Vase fabric: 11, 12, and 13.
Flower fabric: 14A through 14E, 15A and 15B.

3 Cut out all the appliqué pieces along the pattern line marked on the paper backing.

4 You will need an extra piece of fabric for the reversible, or two-sided, appliqué pieces, which include pattern pieces 16 and 17, as well as 14C, 14D, and 14E: Turn the master pattern over, trace the pattern piece on the paper backing, then rough-cut the shape from the fusible web. Fuse the shape to the back of the fabric. Finally, cut the shape out along the pencil line. You should now have two opposite pieces of the same pattern. (Keep these together; you will be fusing them, wrong sides together, in later steps.)

FUSING THE BASIC NO-SEW PIECES

1 Arrange each leaf piece, except 16 and 17, on the background fabric. (Wait to remove the paper backing until you've placed the individual piece; otherwise, you may have trouble identifying it for placement.) Use the green shaded areas in Figure 2-5 as a guide: Place pattern piece 1 first, then pattern piece 2, and so on. Overlap the edges of adjoining pieces 1/16″ to 1/8″. When you are happy with the arrangement, fuse the leaves in place.

2 Remove the paper backing from the vase pieces and arrange them on the background. (Eliminate piece 12 if your fabric is not transparent.) Then fuse the vase in place.

3 Remove the backing from 14A, 14B, and 15A, arrange them on the background, and fuse them in place.

MAKING THE FREE-FORM FLOWERS

The free-form petals in this design have wire mesh fused between two layers of fabric so they can be shaped. (See "Dimensional Appliqué" earlier in this chapter for more on creating three-dimensional shapes. For additional information on reversible fabric, refer to "Leaves" in the directions for the *Full-Blown Flowers Block* in Chapter 3.)

1 Start with the paired pieces you cut out for 14C, 14D, and 14E. Cut out a piece of aluminum screening or mesh that is 1/4″ to 1/8″ smaller than each shape, so the screen won't extend beyond the fabric when it is fused between the two layers.

2 Remove the paper backing from the cut-out fabric shapes, and place the screening or mesh between the two fabrics. (Be sure you put the fabric pieces back-to-back, or wrong sides together.) Center the screening and fuse them all together. Trim around the edges to neaten the shapes, if necessary. Bend to shape the mesh.

3 Apply a dab of fabric glue to the center of each petal, then attach the petals to the background fabric, following the pattern.

MAKING THE PADDED FLOWER

The main part of the right-hand flower in this hanging is padded with fusible fleece to create a three-dimensional effect. Here's how to make it:

1 Take the pattern piece you cut out for 15B, and cut out a piece of fusible fleece 1/8″ to 1/4″ smaller than the shape.

2 Position the fleece on the background fabric. Remove the paper backing from the appliqué shape, and place the shape over the fleece. Overlap the stem (piece 10) by 1/8″. When you are happy with the arrangement, fuse them all in place.

3 To make sure the bond is secure, press from the back as well.

FINISHING UP

1 To make the free-form leaf (pattern piece 16) and the flower bud at the top of the hanging (pattern piece 17), use the paired pieces you cut out, and follow the directions above for making the free-form flower petals (14C, 14D, and 14E). To make the leaf stand out from the hanging, use florist's wire between the layers. Pad the flower bud with fleece.

2 To make the stamens, take paper- or fabric-wrapped florist's wire and color it with a fabric marker. Fuse black reversible fabric to the ends. Apply fabric glue to the base of each piece, then attach them to the background fabric.

3 To finish the center block, place the backing, right side down, on a flat surface. Place the batting on top of it, then center the appliquéd top on the batting. Baste and machine-quilt through the layers in a free-form pattern. The mosaic border, covered in the next section, can be added before quilting the piece.

Mosaic Appliqué Frame

The frame for the Vase with Lilies Wall Hanging *features mosaic appliqué, a great technique for putting scraps of fabric to use. (See "Design Ideas—Mosaic Appliqué" earlier in this chapter for more ideas on using this versatile technique.) Note that the batting and backing fabric for this project are included in the Fabric and Supplies list for the* Vase with Lilies Wall Hanging.

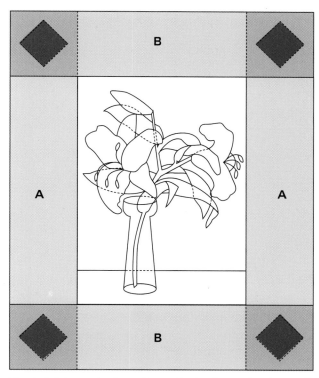

Fig. 2-6. Mosaic Appliqué Frame *for the* Vase with Lilies Wall Hanging

Finished Size. 18″ × 22″.

Techniques. Mosaic appliqué, basic no-sew appliqué.

FABRIC AND SUPPLIES

⅔ yd. cream fabric for background of border

Scraps of miscellaneous fabric for mosaic shapes

½ yd. paper-backed fusible web

Paper or cardboard for diamond template

18″ × 22″ canvas stretchers

CREATING THE MOSAIC FRAME

1 Cut two 6″ × 14″ strips for A, and two 6″ × 22″ strips for B (Fig. 2-6). The finished border is 4″ wide; the additional 2″ on each side are for stretching around canvas stretchers for display.

2 Join the A strips, then the B strips, to the *Vase with Lilies* center panel. (You can either fuse or sew the strips.)

3 Cut a 2″ square out of paper or cardboard to use as a template for the diamond pattern in each corner.

4 Mark the diamond on the frame border lightly in pencil, as a guide for adding the mosaic pieces.

5 Fuse paper-backed fusible web onto the wrong side of the mosaic fabrics. Then cut the fabric into ½″ squares. The quickest way to do this is to cut strips, then cut the strips into squares (or any other shapes you'd like to use). Remove the paper backing from the shapes and fuse them to the frame in a pleasing arrangement.

FINISHING UP

Mount the finished wall hanging using 18″ × 22″ canvas stretchers. (See "Displaying Your Work" in Chapter 7 for instructions.)

Art Nouveau Stained Glass Window

This project features a simple design, but the right fabrics turn it into a real eye-catcher! The flowers, diamonds, and leaves are made from a cotton fabric with metallic threads woven through it; the threads reflect light much like glass. For the background, I layered organdy on top of a 100-percent cotton batting that was scrunched and then sprayed with gold dye to produce a mottled effect, like real stained glass.

Fig. 2-7. Art Nouveau Stained Glass Window

Finished Size. 16″ × 24″.
Techniques. Stained glass appliqué,
basic no-sew appliqué.
Pattern. Pages 117–120.

FABRIC AND SUPPLIES

½ yd. cream organdy for background

½ yd. black fabric for leading

⅛ yd. or scraps of red fabric for flowers and diamonds

⅛ yd. or scraps of green fabric for leaves

½ yd. backing fabric

18″ × 26″ piece of cotton batting

2½ yds. binding

1 yd. paper-backed fusible web

MAKING THE LEADED DESIGN

1 Trace the design from the actual size pattern to create a master pattern. (Remember to reverse the design.)

2 Trace from the master pattern onto the back of paper-backed fusible web.

3 Fuse the web piece to the back of the black fabric, then cut the design out carefully. To prevent the paper backing from separating from the fusible web, cut out the *lead* design in one work session. While cutting out the design, turn the fabric often so you can cut around the curves and corners more easily.

4 Set the leaded design aside to fuse later.

MAKING THE FLOWERS, DIAMONDS, AND LEAVES

1 Write a letter indicating the color of each shape on the master pattern and each appliqué piece. (R for red; G for green.) Then trace the appliqué shapes onto the back of paper-backed fusible web. To avoid a gap between the appliqué shapes and the leading in the finished design, make the appliqués slightly larger than the original shapes, by drawing approximately ⅛₆″ to ⅛″ beyond each shape.

2 Using Figure 2-7 as a guide, fuse the appropriate shapes to the back side of the red and green fabrics.

3 Cut the appliqué shapes out carefully.

4 Following the pattern, fuse the appliqués in place on the background fabric.

FINISHING UP

1 Fuse the leaded design on top of the appliqués, following the pattern.

2 Place the backing, right side down, on a flat surface. Place the batting on top of it, then center the appliqued top on the batting.

3 Quilt along the leaded design, stitching on the cream fabric only. Leaving the colored fabric areas unquilted will make them stand out visually.

4 Trim the edges to 16″ × 24″.

5 Fuse or sew the binding on. See Chapter 7 for information on binding techniques.

Pinwheel Window Curtain

Window treatments are among the easiest home decorating projects to make or decorate. They are versatile, too. For example, they can add style to a room, disguise a dreary view, or provide a focal point in a room.

This project demonstrates several ways you can use shadow appliqué: Sheers and opaque fabrics are combined to create both solid and translucent images. First, triangles are arranged on a plain purchased curtain to produce various patterns. After the design is fused in place, the entire curtain is covered with a sheer fabric. Finally, twisted cord is glued in a free-form pattern on top of the sheer fabric.

Finished Size. 44″ × 78″.

Techniques. Shadow appliqué, basic no-sew appliqué.

FABRIC AND SUPPLIES

44″ × 78″ purchased cotton curtain

¼ yd. of each of the fabrics listed in the Cutting Chart

2½ yds. of 48″ to 54″ wide tulle for the sheer overlay

14 yds. twisted cord

1 yd. fine fusible web

1 yd. paper-backed fusible web

7 yds. of ⅜″ paper-backed fusible web tape

Fabric glue

Liquid fray preventative

Teflon or nonstick press sheet

1 Fuse fine fusible web onto the tulle. (Since fine fusible web is not paper-backed, you'll need to use a Teflon or nonstick press sheet.)

2 Fuse paper-backed fusible web onto the wrong side of the cotton fabrics listed in the Cutting Chart (page 22). Then cut out the number of triangles listed.

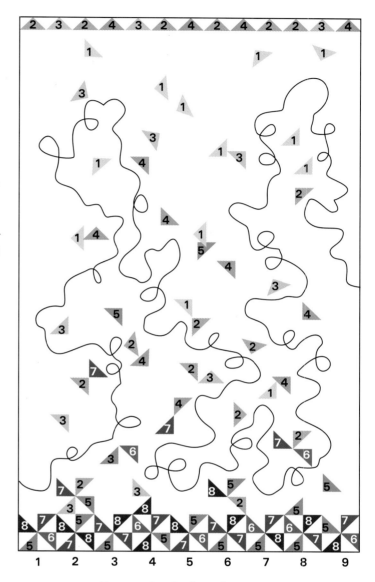

Fig. 2-8. Pinwheel Window Curtain

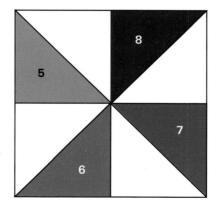

Fig. 2-9. *A sample pinwheel pattern block*

CUTTING CHART

To make the triangles for this project, apply paper-backed fusible web to the wrong side of the fabric, using fine web for the tulle, and heavier web for the cottons. To make triangles, first cut the fabrics into 2½″ squares, then cut the squares across the diagonal to create the required number of triangles.

FABRIC COLOR	TRIANGLES NEEDED
Color 1: light blue tulle	7 squares; 13 triangles
Color 2: medium blue tulle	8 squares; 16 triangles
Color 3: medium turquoise tulle	6 squares; 12 triangles
Color 4: medium forest tulle	6 squares; 12 triangles
Color 5: light turquoise cotton	8 squares; 16 triangles
Color 6: medium seafoam cotton	4 squares; 8 triangles
Color 7: medium turquoise cotton	5 squares; 15 triangles
Color 8: cobalt blue cotton	6 squares; 12 triangles

3   Spread the cotton curtain out on a flat surface. Remove the paper backing from the triangles. Beginning at the top of the curtain, just below where the row of triangles will run across the very top, arrange the triangles in a pattern. I used more triangles at the bottom, where I arranged them in a pinwheel pattern. If you would like to use the same design, refer to Figure 2-8 as a guide for placing the various colors; refer to Figure 2-9 to construct the pinwheels. (There are nine pinwheel pattern blocks across the bottom.)

4   When you are happy with the arrangement, fuse the triangles in place. (Be sure to use the nonstick press sheet when fusing the sheers.)

5   Center the length of tulle on top of the entire curtain. (The tulle should be at least 2″ larger on each side than the curtain.) Pin in place to secure.

6   Check for any strings or stray threads between the tulle and the curtain. (If you discover any after the piece is completed, use tweezers to remove them.) Then, using fine fusible web tape and a nonstick press sheet, fuse one side of the tulle to the curtain along the edges. Repeat on the other side, then the top and the bottom. As you fuse each side, check to be sure the tulle is lying flat against the curtain; sheer fabric has a tendency to slip and bunch up easily.

7   After the tulle is fused in place, add the row of triangles across the top.

8   Carefully trim the excess tulle along each edge.

9   Arrange the cording any way you like on the curtain. When you are happy with the arrangement, glue the cording in place with fabric glue. Or, if you prefer, you can quilt the design instead—try using a decorative machine stitch. When quilting shadow appliqué, work from the center of the piece outward, to prevent the top layer from shifting.

10   If the curtain needs pressing, be sure to cover the sheer fabric with a press cloth to prevent scorching.

CHAPTER 3

FABRIC MANIPULATION

As any quilter knows, fabric is "paint." It contributes color and texture to every piece you create. Once you look beyond its flat, two-dimensional qualities, though, the possibilities for even the most uninteresting piece of fabric are endless. This chapter explores the many ways ordinary fabric can be reshaped and sculpted to create an exciting array of special effects. In the pages that follow, you will find examples of simple, no-sew methods for manipulating fabric that add a whole new dimension of texture, visual interest, and shape to a variety of projects. These range from techniques for altering raw edges—fringing, fraying, and burning, for example—to methods for reshaping fabric, such as scrunching, gathering, stretching, pleating, folding, and even weaving, braiding, and twisting.

If there is one key to success with these techniques, it is experimentation. Every fabric responds differently to a particular technique. For example, there are pliable fabrics, like chiffon and organza, which drape well, or fall into soft curves when folded. Crisper fabrics, such as linen, poplin, and taffeta, can be pleated and folded accurately. Some knitted and rayon fabrics are stretchy; some linens and wools have very loose weaves. For best results, test different fabrics with each technique to see exactly how they will respond.

The projects in this chapter are adaptations from the elegant Baltimore Album-style quilts. (All the projects are blocks from the *Way-Beyond Baltimore Album Quilt*, assembled in Chapter 7.) Each block is designed to illustrate many different fabric manipulation techniques and how they can be used. You may want to start with just one or two techniques, and then experiment with the others as you gain confidence. Don't be intimidated: You will find the projects surprisingly easy.

MANIPULATING RAW EDGES

Fringing, fraying, burning, and serrating the raw edges of a piece of fabric are marvelous ways to add dimension, texture, interest, and shape to a project. Each method creates a different effect: Fraying and fringing give the piece a feathery look; burning results in a soft-looking edge; and serrating an edge with pinking shears creates an ornamental, zigzag effect. The *Pennsylvania Dutch Flowers Block* illustrates a variety of ways raw edges can be manipulated.

As with all the techniques in this chapter, you will learn a great deal by experimenting with different fabrics. For example, the raw edges of most fab-

Pennsylvania Dutch Flowers Block. *The flowers and foliage on this block from the* Way-Beyond Baltimore Album Quilt *are created using a variety of techniques for manipulating raw edges, including serrating, burning, fringing, and fraying. Directions for this project begin on page 31.*

Pennsylvania Dutch Flowers Materials. *These fabrics and materials from the* Pennsylvania Dutch Flowers Block *take on a whole new look when their raw edges are altered by techniques like fringing, fraying, serrating, and burning.*

rics fray, but the edges of some nonwoven fabrics—such as felt, leather, Ultrasuede, and interfacings—do not. If you want to keep an edge from fraying, you can seal it with liquid fray preventative, fabric glue, or fusible web. Burning the edges also prevents fraying. On the other hand, fringing and fraying can add interest. Upholstery-type fabrics and denim, which generally have different-colored warp and weft threads, are especially suitable for fringing or fraying. You can also stiffen the edges of a piece of fabric—for example, by applying white glue or brush-on fabric stiffener, then molding the fabric edge into a shape and allowing it to dry.

Fringing

There are a variety of ways to use fringe in a project. For example, you can use it as edging, or wrap and tie it to form a tassel. Pieces of fringe can be overlapped to add weight and dimension. Stringing beads on the ends of fringes is a fun way to add color and excitement to a piece. The *Pennsylvania Dutch Flowers Block* features flowers made from purchased thread fringe, as well as hand-cut fabric and loop fringe.

To make hand-cut fringe from a piece of fabric, first determine the length of fringe you need. Keep in mind that you will need to double the finished width, since the fabric will be folded in half. Fold a strip of fabric lengthwise, wrong sides together. (Bias-cut fabric works well for this type of fringing. Jersey knit fabric not only fringes nicely, it curls, too.) You can fold it either in half or off-center; an off-center fold will give the fringe more dimension. To form the fringe, make parallel cuts into either the folded edge or the cut edge; the end you cut will depend on whether you want loops or open fringe. (For more details, see the step-by-step directions for the Fabric Loop Fringe Flower and the Fabric Fringe Flower in the *Pennsylvania Dutch Flowers Block* beginning on page 33.) If you are making rows of fringe, draw parallel lines on your background fabric as a guide for placing your rows, allowing for overlap of the previous row.

Fraying

Fraying is a very simple technique that softens the look of a raw edge and adds visual interest, dimension, and texture. Rayon, chiffon, and organza-type fabrics fray in a wonderful, feathery fashion. Although most fabrics can be frayed, some—such as felt, Ultrasuede, leather, and nonwoven interfacing—cannot. Bias-cut raw edges generally do not fray too much.

To fray fabric, simply rub it between your fingers, scratch it with your fingernails, or brush over the edges with a toothbrush. Sometimes lightly spraying the fabric with water and then rubbing it works well. You'll have to experiment, since some fabrics fray better than others.

Burning

Burning can create a natural, pliable-looking edge that is especially effective when used to represent images such as clouds or flower petals. It is best to work with natural fibers, since synthetics can burst into flames very easily. Silk singes nicely; cotton is more flammable. Rayon goes up in flames! Fabrics containing polyester tend to melt, resulting in a unique finish.

To ensure safety, work on a Teflon or nonstick press sheet, or place the candle securely in a tray of water, in case any ashes fall. Cut the shape out of the fabric, allowing about ¼" of extra fabric around the shape. Hold the fabric with tweezers or needle-nose pliers and carefully put it in the flame, burning it along the edge.

FABRIC MANIPULATION

♦ The texture created by manipulating fabric responds to light and shadow. Many "texturized" fabrics appear solid from a distance, but up close they reveal a profusion of details, generating special effects.

♦ Keep in mind that many of these techniques use at least twice the amount of fabric you would ordinarily need for a two-dimensional design.

♦ Manipulated fabrics are usually difficult to quilt. Use other methods, such as tying or knotting, and add embellishments or decorative stitches before attaching the batting and backing.

♦ Try layering fabrics that have been manipulated. Layering, which involves stacking one piece or shape of fabric on top of the other, adds additional texture, depth, and dimension. Increasing or decreasing the size of each layer provides even more texture and dimension. Try layering unusual fabrics like sheers, textures, open weaves, satin, and shiny or transparent fabrics.

♦ Although the results are *not* always predictable, it is well worth using fabric manipulation techniques.

Not all fabrics respond to burning in the same way. Some have a charred look; others bead along the edge. Since some fabrics can burst into flames, always test a small sample piece. Be extremely careful when using this technique: Always work in a well-ventilated room with a fire extinguisher or water—or both—nearby.

Serrating

Another simple way to reshape an edge is to serrate, perforate, or cut it to make a zigzag, wavy, or other decorative design. Cutting edges of fabric with pinking shears can help prevent fraying, produce a decorative finish, or even create a pictorial image. Decorative rotary blades, including pinking blades and wave blades, are also available.

SCRUNCHING, WRINKLING, STRETCHING, AND GATHERING

Fabric manipulation techniques such as scrunching, wrinkling, stretching, and gathering are useful for changing the surface texture of fabric. They also add

Full-Blown Flowers Block. *Dimensional appliqué leaves complement a textured basket made from scrunched fabric on this block from the Way-Beyond Baltimore Album Quilt. The rich array of flowers are created using various fabric manipulation techniques, such as gathering and stretching. Directions for this project begin on page 36.*

Full-Blown Flowers Materials. *Fabric manipulation techniques like scrunching, gathering, and stretching allow you to transform flat fabric, various trims, and ordinary wire-edge ribbon into an extraordinary variety of textures and shapes.*

dimension to a project. The *Full-Blown Flowers Block* uses a variety of fabric manipulation techniques to create both the flowers and the basket they are arranged in. (See the step-by-step instructions beginning on page 36 for more details on these techniques.)

As you try these techniques, experiment with a variety of fabrics. For example, try gathering or scrunching velvet, then do the same thing with a sheer fabric. Or experiment with fabrics cut on the bias. You'll find they react differently than fabrics cut on the straight grain; generally, bias-cut fabrics are more pliable and fray less. Keep in mind that each fabric responds to manipulation in a distinct way. And don't forget that you can combine these techniques with others in the book to create your own unique effects. For instance, try fraying or fringing the edges of fabric before you gather it.

Scrunching and Wrinkling

"Scrunching" a fabric means crushing or crunching it, while "wrinkling" a fabric means creating ridges or furrows by crumpling, folding, and shrinking it. Since both scrunching and wrinkling affect pattern and color placement, the result is a totally different design and texture—Like magic, you have a brand new fabric! By using these easy, effective techniques, you can recreate and reshape some of those out-of-date fabrics that have accumulated in your closet.

Check the fiber content before scrunching and wrinkling fabric. Natural fibers, including linen and 100-percent cotton, generally provide the best results because they hold creases well. Some poly-blends also respond well to these techniques. Many synthetics, on the other hand, will not retain a sharp crease. Test various fabrics to see how scrunching or wrinkling affects them. Also, think about what you've observed when you sew or do the laundry: Which clothing wrinkles the most? Are there any frayed seams on those linen pants?

Both scrunching and wrinkling effectively "shrink" the fabric, so when using these techniques, be sure to allow up to two or three times more fabric than the final amount required. Remember: It is always better to have too much fabric for your project than not enough.

To scrunch a piece of fabric, begin by prewashing it. Then, while it is still wet, take each end of the fabric and twist it tightly as if you were wringing it out (Fig. 3-1). Starting at one end, tie the twisted fabric tightly from one end to the other with string.

Tumble dry with towels for at least an hour, then let it air dry, preferably in a warm place. Keep it tied until it is thoroughly dry. (Depending on the fabric and where you put it, this could take a day or two.) Then remove the string and fuse the fabric to interfacing or paper-backed fusible web to hold the scrunching in place.

Fig. 3-1. *To scrunch fabric, prewash it, then twist it until it turns back on itself. Tie the twists in place and dry.*

Here's an even easier way to scrunch: Prewash the fabric, twist or crunch it into a tight ball, then stuff it into the toe of a nylon stocking. Tie securely and tumble dry. When it's completely dry, fuse the fabric to interfacing or paper-backed fusible web to hold the scrunching in place.

To wrinkle a piece of fabric, simply dampen it, crunch it into a smaller size, then place a hot iron directly on top to set the wrinkles. (Do not move the iron from side to side, or you'll remove the wrinkles.) Fuse the fabric to interfacing or paper-backed fusible web to hold the wrinkles in place.

Stretching

Another way to reshape fabric is by stretching it. This technique creates an interesting—and totally different—effect, giving shape and texture to edges. Only certain fabrics will stretch successfully. Knits respond very well; cotton jersey knits work best. (Some jersey knits contain Lycra, which tends to cause the fabric to return to its original shape.) Stretching can add attractive accents to various forms found in nature, such as the bends and turns of a flower petal. This technique can also give gentle movement to a piece, like sand dunes.

To stretch a piece of knit fabric, spray the edges generously with water. With your left hand, pinch the edge of the fabric between your thumb and forefinger. Do the same thing with your right hand, about 1″ from your left hand. Stretch the fabric by pushing it with your left hand and pulling with your right. Repeat down the entire length of the strip and then on the other edge. Allow the fabric to dry.

Gathering

Gathering is a very versatile technique that can be used with nearly any type of fabric, including ribbons and trims. Traditionally, it is done by sewing two lines of running stitches along the edge of the fabric, tying them off at one end, and then pulling the threads along the top of the fabric while gently arranging the puckers or ruffles that result along the length of the fabric. The fullness of the gathers is determined by the initial length of the fabric. Generally, you need a piece of fabric 1½ to 3 times longer/wider/larger than the finished piece; two times, or double, is the average.

There are a variety of gathered trims and ribbons you can use to make no-sew flowers and other ornaments quickly and easily. For instance, many of the flowers in the *Full-Blown Flowers Block* are made using purchased, pregathered items, including heat-set gathered ribbon and box-pleated trim. Wire-edge ribbon can also be gathered quite easily, with spectacular results. (For more on using these materials to make flowers, see the step-by-step directions beginning on page 36.)

PLEATING, FOLDING, AND ROLLING

Pleating, folding, and rolling are especially useful for adding dimension and creating natural-looking forms like feathers and flowers. The pleated vase and folded flowers in the *Morning Glory Block* illustrate some of the ways in which these techniques can be used.

Pleating

Dressmakers commonly use pleats when making skirts and other clothing, but pleating offers creative opportunities for quilters as well. Pleating or tucking a piece of fabric produces folds that create a pattern of light and shadow. Fabrics that have been pleated or tucked can be used to represent natural features like ripples in a pond or the texture of a field. They are also useful for simulating architectural features such as clapboards on a house.

Pleats and tucks are similar and are formed in the same manner, by doubling the fabric back on itself and pressing the fold into place. In dressmaking, a pleat (in a skirt, for instance) is open on one end and can be both decorative and functional. A tuck (say, in a blouse) is sewn closed at both ends and is always used as a decorative element. The way the fabric is folded determines the type of pleat. A fan is an

Morning Glory Block. *Pleating and folding, the featured techniques in this elegant block, are ideal for forming natural-looking textures and shapes such as bird feathers and flower buds. The morning glory is made from fabric that is folded origami-style. Directions for this project begin on page 43.*

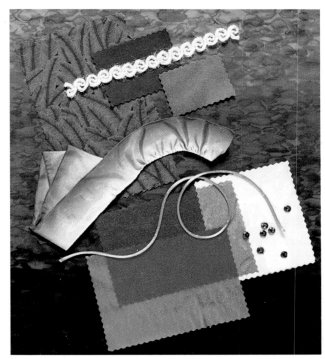

Morning Glory Materials. *Wire-edge ribbon is folded and rolled to form the flower buds on the Morning Glory Block. Folding and pleating fabrics are ideal techniques for add dimension and patterns of light and shadow to change fabrics used in projects.*

example of an accordion pleat. Most pleated skirts have knife pleats, which are made from folds that face the same direction. Box pleats, on the other hand, are created from folds that turn in opposite directions.

The look and texture of pleats can vary greatly, depending on the weight of the fabric, the width of the pleats, and so forth. Leaving pleats unpressed can result in a softer, more rounded effect. The fiber content of a fabric influences how sharp and crisp the pleat appears. Crisp, firmly woven fabrics are the best choice for pleating and tucking, because they fold easily and hold pleats well. Suitable fabrics include fine cottons, handkerchief linens, batiste, as well as organza.

Stripes are great for pleating. Try taking a two-color striped fabric, with both stripes the same width. Fold along the outside edge of a stripe (this will become the predominant color of the fabric) to the inside edge of the next stripe of the same color. Continue folding until the entire width of the fabric is pleated. Next, fold the pleats from side to side in an irregular fashion to create the illusion of constant movement, or fold them to create a geometric form, such as a diamond pattern. Experiment with your sample, and think about ways you can use pleated fabric to represent certain images. Consider which objects in nature could be symbolized by pleated fabric—ripples in the sand, waves on the sea, bird feathers, or tree bark, for example.

The easiest way to make pleats is to use a tool called a Perfect Pleater, which can create uniform pleats in minutes, with no measuring required. There are only two steps: Tuck the pleats in place, then press to set. When pleating, keep in mind that you will need two to three times more fabric than you would ordinarily.

You can also pleat by hand, although it takes a little time to mark the fabric. To make ¼″ knife pleats, for example, mark your fabric as shown in Figure 3-2, then fold and press, as shown in Figure 3-3. To make different-size pleats, adjust the width of the markings. You can use straight pins, hair clips, bobby pins, or clothespins to hold pleats and folds in place as you are gluing a pleated piece to a background fabric.

Folding

The technique of folding fabric can be as simple or as complex as you want it to be. A piece of fabric can simply be folded in half, or it can be manipulated using the techniques of origami, the Japanese art of folding paper. Some of the less complicated origami folds can be easily modified for fabric. For best results, practice with paper before you begin folding

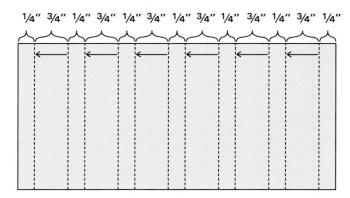

Fig. 3-2. *To make pleats by hand, mark the top and bottom of the fabric to be pleated. For ¼″ pleats, mark at alternating intervals of ¼″ and ¾″. Always measure from the previous mark. The second mark is the fold line.*

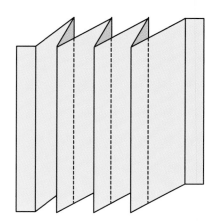

Fig. 3-3. *After marking the fabric, fold it in the direction of the arrow to the first mark to form the pleats. Pin at the top and bottom; steam press in place as you go. Dampen a press cloth with a mixture of one part white vinegar to nine parts water, place it on the pleated fabric, then steam set.*

fabric. Tightly woven natural fibers are easiest to work with and retain folds the best. Light- to medium-weight fabrics—organza, handkerchief linen, and cotton batiste, for example—are the most suitable for this technique. You can also fuse two lightweight fabrics like nylon and metallic lamé. (Combining two different fabrics—wrong sides together—gives you the opportunity to work with two distinct colors. Fusing fabrics also prevents fraying, since it seals the edges.) Some types of ribbon can be folded, although grosgrain ribbon doesn't hold a crease very well, and satin ribbon frays easily.

Rolling

Rolling is a technique featured in several of the projects in this chapter, and is as simple as its name suggests. It is especially useful for making flower buds; pieces of fabric or ribbon can be rolled to create a variety of buds and partially opened flowers. The flower buds on the *Morning Glory Block* are folded first and then rolled. Fabric or ribbon can also be wrapped around itself, or around something else. For example, to create lifelike flowers, you can wrap the petal fabric around fringed stamens.

WEAVING, BRAIDING, KNOTTING, AND COILING

These simple techniques are very familiar to most crafters. After all, who hasn't braided hair or woven paper strips together to make a place mat in grade school? And if you've ever made a braided rug, you have used both braiding and coiling methods. There are countless ways you can use these techniques to create unique and striking effects of color, pattern, and texture in no-sew projects. For instance, you can put accumulated scraps to use by cutting them into strips, then knotting, sewing, or fusing them together. The strips can then be woven together, or braided and coiled, to create an entirely new piece of fabric. (To avoid fraying when working with twisted cords and trims, wrap tape around the cord, then cut through the tape.) The *Woven Basket of Flowers Block* shows how woven fabric strips or ribbon can be used to create unique no-sew special effects.

As with other methods of fabric manipulation, weaving, braiding, knotting, and coiling break up the

Woven Basket of Flowers Materials. *Torn strips of fabric, decorative thread, and ribbons can be used to create a fascinating array of shapes and forms.*

Woven Basket of Flowers Block. *Weaving, braiding, and knotting are simple techniques that yield spectacular results. The basket and several of the flowers on this block illustrate many different weaving methods that are both fun and easy to learn. Directions for this project begin on page 49.*

pattern on a piece of fabric. All of these techniques soften the edges and blend the colors of the different fabrics. As you use each method, notice the interplay of color and light, giving the fabrics a dimensional feel, as well as added texture.

Weaving

There are countless patterns and types of weaves, but the most familiar is the plain weave, made by following the "one over, one under" rule we all learned in grade school. If two colors are used, the result is a checkerboard pattern. Quilters can weave fabric for the sole purpose of cutting it up for a specific shape, or make an entire quilt by weaving strips of fabric together. (For details on several different weaving techniques, see the step-by-step directions for the *Woven Basket of Flowers Block* beginning on page 49.)

Fabric, ribbons, Ultrasuede, and dressmaking or upholstery trims can all be used for fast, easy weaving. Once you've made a weaving, you can fuse interfacing or paper-back fusible web on the back to create a fabric, then cut it up and use it as you wish.

EXTRA-EASY WEAVING

Remember when you made place mats from construction paper in first grade? You can use the same technique in no-sew appliqué. This technique is especially easy and effective with fabrics or other materials that do not fray or that fray very little, such as canvas, Ultrasuede, and leather. Take a solid piece of nonwoven or tightly woven fabric, and cut it larger than the pattern shape. Measure and mark the warp. Make parallel cuts in the fabric to form the warp. End the cut lines at least 1" from the top and bottom of the fabric. (Try to have an odd number of strips so the edges are the same on both sides.) Then start to weave the weft through the warp (Fig. 3-4). To stabilize the weaving, fuse lightweight interfacing or paper-backed fusible web on the back.

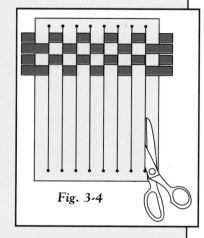

Fig. 3-4

Braiding

Braiding is a very quick technique that can be used to create a customized trim for a specific project. A braid can also be applied to the surface with fabric glue to accent a shape, draw a line, or outline a form. Or, you can place braids in rows to form a shape, or coil them. In addition to braiding fabric scraps, try braiding different ribbons and trims of similar widths to create interesting new trims. The basket handle and flower stems on the *Woven Basket of Flowers Block* illustrate different types of braids.

Knotting

Knotting is a practical way to connect cords, ribbons, or ropes together, or to keep something—say, a thread—in place. But you can also use knots to create distinctive flowers and other shapes. Combining strips of different fabrics using knots can yield interesting results. For example, the Knotted Bluebells on the *Woven Basket of Flowers Block* are made from strips of light and dark blue fabric knotted together. The Knotted Zinnia is created by making a series of knots in a strip of fabric, then rolling them up and gluing them in place. Just use your imagination, and experiment with the different shapes you can create with knots. You'll find a wealth of ways to intermingle the colors of fabrics and add dimension to a piece.

Coiling

Coiling is useful for shaping circles, ovals, and even baskets. The beautiful coiled baskets of native Americans are one of the best examples of this technique combined with exquisite design. The center of the Coiled, Looped Sunflower on the *Woven Basket of Flowers Block* is made by simply coiling a piece of cording and gluing it in place. Consider coiling other materials, too. For example, an open zipper would create a unique texture, or try coiling various trims to produce unusual shapes and textures for a piece.

WARM UP WITH GREETING CARDS

Fabric manipulation techniques lend themselves to creating small works of art for your family and friends. Why not try your hand at making your own cards for Valentine's Day and other special occasions? Begin with blank, folded greeting cards with square, oval, or rectangular windows already cut out. (Some of these have a remountable adhesive inside for easy assembly.) Use materials like wire-edge ribbon to make a gathered rose, or pleat a unique fabric to make a fancy fan. This is a great way to tell others you think they are special, while learning some new techniques to add to your repertoire.

Pennsylvania Dutch Flowers Block

This block features several ways that manipulated edges can be used to add shape, interest, texture, and dimension to a project. The raw edges on the ferns are fringed and frayed to create a feathery texture. The flowers are created using a variety of techniques: Four flowers are made from various types of fringe—thread fringe, fabric fringe, and fabric loop fringe. Another flower has burned edges, and two others simulate traditional "yoyos" with serrated fabric edges. Layering is used on the fringed ferns as well as several of the flowers, including the serrated yoyos, to give the block even more dimensional appeal. Use Figure 3-5 as a guide to the various parts of the block, referred to in the step-by-step instructions that follow.

FABRIC AND SUPPLIES

13″ x 16″ dark plum fabric for background fabric

¼ yd. medium green print for leaf and calyx fabric

¼ yd. dark teal fabric for Frayed Ferns

¼ yd. medium teal fabric for Frayed Ferns

¼ yd. light teal fabric for Frayed Ferns

Scraps of three coordinating fabrics for Serrated Faux Yoyo Flowers

2 pieces of 2½″ x 5″ fabric for Fabric Loop Fringe and Fabric Fringe Flowers

3″ of 1½″ wide thread fringe for Thread Fringe Flowers

Scraps of silk for Burned-Edge Flower

1 yd. teal 4mm silk ribbon or ⅛″ ribbon for stems

½ yd. yellow 4mm silk ribbon or other ⅛″ ribbon for Fabric Loop Fringe and Fabric Fringe Flower stamens

2″ of braided cord for Burned-Edge Flower stamen

Beads or other embellishments for Burned-Edge Flower

Rivets (⅜″) or other embellishments for Serrated Faux Yoyo Flowers

½ yd. paper-backed fusible web

1 yd. of ⅜″ paper-backed fusible web tape

Fabric glue

Liquid fray preventative

Freezer paper

Rotary cutter with wavy blade

Pinking shears

Drafting tape or heat-resistant tape

Embroidery floss or clear monofilament thread

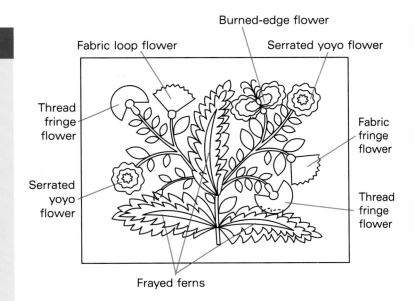

Fig. 3-5. Pennsylvania Dutch Flowers Block

Finished Size. Block: 12″ x 15″. This is Block D from the *Way-Beyond Baltimore Album Quilt*, which is 38″ x 44″.

Techniques. Fringing, fraying, burning, and serrating raw edges, as well as basic no-sew appliqué and dimensional appliqué (described in Chapter 2).

Pattern. Page 121.

STEMS AND LEAVES

1 Make the stems first. Cut the teal silk ribbon to size according to the pattern. To cover the raw edges of the stems, fuse or glue the side stems onto the background fabric first, then attach the main stems. (For example, on the left side of the block are

side stems to the Fabric Loop Fringe Flower and a Serrated Faux Yoyo Flower; the main stem, to the Thread Fringe Flower, should cover the bases of the side stems.) Finally, place the main stem for the bouquet, which runs to the upright Frayed Fern. Seal the bottom edge of the ribbon for the main stem with liquid fray preventative.

2 Using the leaf templates in Figure 3-6, trace the leaves onto paper-backed fusible web. Trace 7 of the large leaves (LL) and 28 of the small leaves (SL). Allow enough space between the leaves to cut around them with pinking shears.

3 Fuse the traced leaves onto the back of the leaf fabric. Cut each leaf from the fabric using pinking shears.

4 Remove the paper backing, then fuse the leaves onto the background fabric along the stems, following the pattern.

5 Trace and fuse the calyxes for all the flowers—except the Serrated Faux Yoyo Flowers—in the same manner as the leaves.

Fig. 3-6.
Leaf templates

FRAYED FERNS

The three fern fronds on this block are layered, using three shades of teal fabric. The largest shape, cut from the dark teal fabric, is on the bottom; the smallest, cut from the light teal fabric, is on the top. Since the ferns are attached to the background fabric in the center only, the back of the fronds will be visible, so try to choose a fabric for the ferns that is dyed rather than printed.

1 To make the ferns, first trace the patterns for all three layers onto the dull side of a sheet of freezer paper. (Use the main pattern for the block on page 121.) Remember to reverse the pattern.

2 Cut the fern patterns from the freezer paper. Then use an iron to press the freezer paper,

shiny side down, onto the back of the fabric the piece is to be cut from. Press the freezer-paper pattern for the three largest fern pieces on the dark teal fabric. Use the medium teal fabric for the medium-sized pieces, and the light teal fabric for the smallest pieces.

3 Cut the ferns out along the pattern line. (Use pinking shears to cut the small center fern shape.) Remove the freezer paper.

4 After cutting out the ferns, fray the edges by rubbing them between your fingers or scratching them with your fingernails.

5 Cut a strip of ³⁄₈″ paper-backed fusible web tape to fit the length of the center of each frond. Fuse the tape onto the center back of each frond. Remove the paper, then fuse the fronds, one layer at a time, onto the background fabric following the pattern.

SERRATED FAUX YOYO FLOWERS

The Serrated Faux Yoyo Flowers are made from circles, and this project demonstrates three different methods for creating and cutting them. The largest circle in each flower is cut with a wavy rotary blade from a piece of two-sided fused fabric (two fabrics with the wrong sides fused together). The middle circle is also cut with a wavy rotary blade, but from a single layer of fabric. (You can use either two-sided, reversible fabric or fabric printed on only one side.) The smallest circle is cut from ribbon with pinking shears. A rivet, which functions as a decorative element as well as a fastening device, is used to attach the layers to the background fabric. Or, if you prefer, you can use other embellishments, such as buttons, for the centers.

1 Start by making a piece of two-sided fused fabric for the large circle. Cut a 2″ square from fabric and fuse it to another piece of fabric, wrong sides together. (I used the same fabric for the front and back, but any two fabrics can be used.) Draw a 1³⁄₄″ circle on the fabric, using Template C in Figure 3-7.

2 Cut the circle out with the wavy rotary blade. To cut, gradually turn the fabric clockwise as

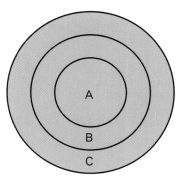

Fig. 3-7. Yoyo flower templates

you slowly move the rotary blade counter-clockwise (Fig. 3-8); you are essentially "pushing" the fabric and the blade together. If you are right-handed, hold the rotary cutter in your right hand and slowly turn the fabric clockwise with your left hand. If you are left-handed, hold the cutter in your left hand and turn the fabric counter-clockwise with your right hand. Another way to cut the circle is to fold a 2″ square of fabric in half, draw a half circle on it, and cut with the wavy rotary cutter, moving the fabric as described above (Fig. 3-9).

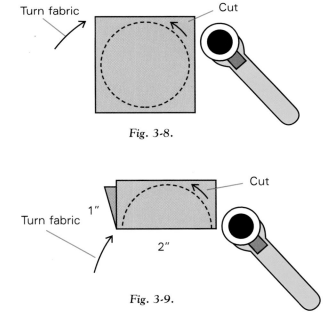

Fig. 3-8.

Fig. 3-9.

3 Repeat Step 2 for the middle circle (Template B, Fig. 3-7), using a 1½″ square of fabric and cutting a 1¼″ circle from it. This circle is cut from a single layer of fabric and will fray, depending on the fabric selected.

4 To make the smallest circle (Template A, Fig. 3-7), cut a ¾″ circle from a 1″ square of ribbon with pinking shears.

5 Attach all the layers with a rivet, button, or other embellishment in the center of the circle. (Tools for attaching are usually included with the rivets.)

FABRIC LOOP FRINGE FLOWER

When you select fabric for the fringe flowers, keep in mind that once the fringe is cut, both sides of the fabric will be visible.

1 To make the fringe for the Fabric Loop Fringe Flower, start with a 2½″ × 5″ piece of fabric. Cut along the length of both 5″ edges with pinking shears to add interest. Fold the fabric in half, wrong sides together (Fig. 3-10). Press the fold.

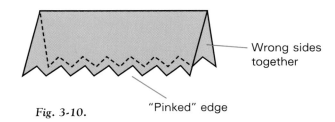

Fig. 3-10.

2 Fuse ⅜″ paper-backed fusible web tape directly along the pinking-sheared edge of the fabric. Remove the paper backing. Bond the wrong sides of the fabric together.

3 Make parallel cuts *on the folded edge* through the two layers of fabric. Cut to the fusible web tape (Fig. 3-11).

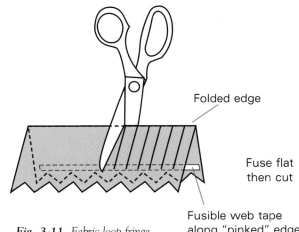

Fig. 3-11. Fabric loop fringe

4 To add the yellow stamens, cut six 1½″ lengths of ribbon. Center them on the inside of the fringed strip and glue them in place (Fig. 3-12).

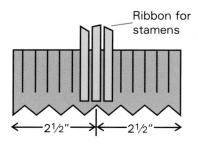

Fig. 3-12.

5 Divide the fringed strip into thirds. Fold the left third over the center, then glue along the bottom edge. Repeat on the right side (Fig. 3-13).

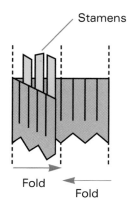

Fig. 3-13.

6 Brush over the fringe with your finger to fluff the fabric loops. Apply glue to the background fabric, then attach one side of the base of the flower. Gather the base by pinching it together with your fingers. Attach the other pinched part to the background fabric, following the pattern. Place a small weight on the base of the flower until the glue sets.

FABRIC FRINGE FLOWER

The Fabric Fringe Flower is made almost exactly the same way as the Fabric Loop Fringe Flower. Take a 2½″ × 5″ piece of fabric, cut along the long edges with pinking shears, then fold the fabric in half length-

wise, wrong sides together. Press the fold. This time, apply the fusible web tape *near the fold* instead of next to the pinking-sheared edge. Remove the paper backing; bond the wrong sides of the fabric together. Make parallel cuts from the pinking-sheared edges up to the fusible web tape near the fold (Fig. 3-14). The result is a strip of open fringe.

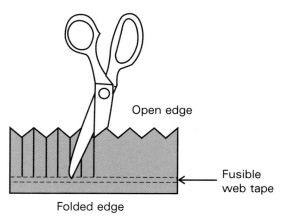

Fig. 3-14. Fabric fringe

THREAD FRINGE FLOWERS

These flowers are made from 1½″-wide ready-made thread fringe that is sewn together across the top. To create a natural-looking color effect, dip the tips of the fringe into dye and let it bleed onto the rest of the fringe. Allow the fringe to dry thoroughly before proceeding. (For more on dyeing, see Chapter 6.)

1 Cut two pieces of thread fringe, each 1½″ long. To prevent the fringe from coming apart, apply glue along the cut edges. Allow the glue to set. Trim the thread fringe to 1″.

2 Apply glue on the back of the fringe along the top (sewn) edge. Attach the fringe to the background fabric, following the pattern.

BURNED-EDGE FLOWER

1 Tape the fabric to the pattern with drafting tape or heat-resistant tape. Trace Templates A, B, and C from Figure 3-15 directly

onto the fabric with chalk or a soft pencil. Cut around the traced line. (Silk and other fine fabrics can be difficult to draw on or cut accurately, since they tend to move around easily. However, you don't need to worry about being precise, since the edges will be burned.)

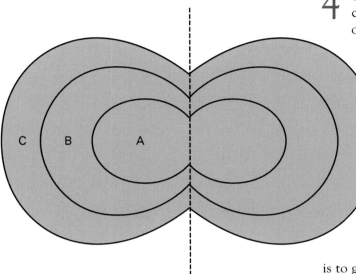

Fig. 3-15. *Burned-edge flower templates*

2 Burn the edges of each shape, following the guidelines provided earlier in this chapter under "Burning."

3 Place a dab of glue in the center of each layer, and glue the layers together.

4 Cut a 2″ piece of matching embroidery floss or clear monofilament thread, then thread a bead or other embellishment on it. Place the bead in the center of the flower, then wrap the thread around the center, knotting the thread on the back of the flower.

5 To add the stamen, cut a 1½″ piece of braided cord. To prevent the cord from unraveling, apply glue at one end. Allow it to dry, then unravel the other end. Glue the sealed end onto the background fabric, following the pattern.

6 Apply glue to the background fabric, in the center of the area where the flower is to go. Attach the flower to the background fabric, following the pattern.

Full-Blown Flowers Block

The Full-Blown Flowers Block illustrates several ways you can use fabric manipulation techniques. The basket is made from scrunched or wrinkled fabric, which adds dimension to an otherwise flat shape and balances the weight of the bouquet of flowers. The flowers are created using a variety of materials and gathering techniques, including wire-edge ribbon, gathered ruffle, box-pleated ribbon trim and heat-set ribbon. When combined, they produce visual interest, along with texture and dimension, for a dazzling effect.

FABRIC AND SUPPLIES

13" × 16" dark plum fabric for background fabric

12" × 18" medium-color fabric for Scrunched Basket

⅓ yd. green sand-washed rayon for leaves

⅓ yd. teal sand-washed rayon for leaves

½ yd. trim for basket

1 yd. of 1½" wide deep rose wire-edge ombre ribbon for Peony

15" salmon crinkled, heat-set ribbon for Zinnias

12" lavender crinkled, heat-set ribbon for Zinnias

10" purple crinkled, heat-set ribbon for Zinnias

15" yellow crinkled, heat-set ribbon for stamens for Zinnias, Hanging Bellflower, and Hollyhock

½ yd. of 1" wide lavender wire-edge ombre ribbon for Rose

½ yd. of 1" wide ruby-red wire-edge ombre ribbon for Rose

⅓ yd. of 1" wide box-pleated ribbon trim for Box-Pleated Ribbon Flower

Scraps of scarlet rayon and a scrap of dark novelty fabric for Poppy stamen

3" of 1½" wide ruffle for Hanging Bellflower

2½" × 8" jersey knit for Hollyhock

14" green cording

6" of 1½" wide thread fringe

3" of ⅜" wide green grosgrain ribbon for Hanging Bellflower calyx

⅓ yd. paper-backed fusible web

Scraps of ⅜" paper-backed fusible web tape

Wire thread or clear monofilament thread

Fabric stiffener

Fabric glue

Liquid fray preventative

Clothespins

The flowers in this block look elaborate, but they are actually very easy to make. You may want to start with just one or two techniques, then try others as you gain confidence. All the flowers are drawn in the same style, so you can use as many or as few techniques as you like. However, keep in mind that the finished flowers will vary slightly in size; if you are drawing your design directly onto the block, mark only the center of the flower. Use Figure 3-16 as a guide to the various parts of the block, referred to in the step-by-step directions that follow.

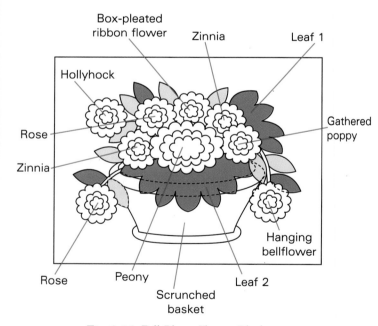

Fig. 3-16. Full-Blown Flowers Block

Finished Size. Block: 12" × 15". This is Block E from the *Way-Beyond Baltimore Album Quilt*, which is 38" × 44".

Techniques. Scrunching or wrinkling, stretching, and gathering fabric, as well as basic no-sew appliqué and dimensional appliqué (described in Chapter 2).

Pattern. Page 122.

SCRUNCHED BASKET

1 Scrunch or wrinkle the fabric for the basket using one of the methods described under "Scrunching and Wrinkling" earlier in this chapter. (A fabric with a marbled or small textural design is very effective; see Chapter 5 for more information on these techniques.) Before fusing the paper-backed fusible web onto the fabric, reverse the pattern and trace it onto the paper side. Then fuse the traced basket shape to the scrunched/wrinkled fabric. Press the iron firmly to melt the webbing into the crevices. For best results, fuse from the back first, then repeat from the front.

2 Cut the fused basket shape out. Remove the paper, then bond the basket to the background fabric following the pattern.

3 Cut 2 lengths of trim for the basket: 12″ for the top edge, and 6″ for the bottom edge. Seal the edges with liquid fray preventative. Glue the trim in place along the top and bottom of the basket.

LEAVES

All the leaves are made from reversible or two-sided fabric. Sand-washed rayon was selected because it is fairly soft and gathers without a lot of bulk, but any fine fabric will work. To give the leaves even more flexibility, the inside of the paper-backed fusible web shape is cut out before the web is bonded to the fabric.

1 Use the leaf shapes in Figure 3-17 as templates and trace them onto paper-backed fusible web. You will need one each of the two larger leaves (Leaf 1 and Leaf 2), and 11 of the small leaves. (The templates for Leaf 1 and

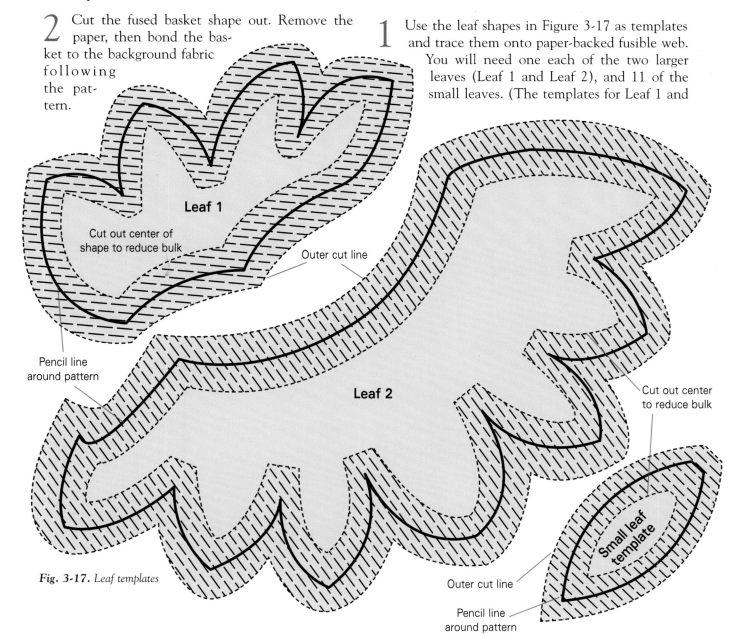

Leaf 1

Cut out center of shape to reduce bulk

Outer cut line

Pencil line around pattern

Leaf 2

Cut out center to reduce bulk

Small leaf template

Outer cut line

Pencil line around pattern

Fig. 3-17. *Leaf templates*

Leaf 2 are already reversed.) Cut around the shapes, ¼″ outside of the pencil line (along outer cut line). Then cut out the center of the shapes to reduce bulk. The resulting shapes are represented by the patterned areas in Figure 3-17.

2 Fuse the web side of all of the leaves to the back side of the green leaf fabric. Cut each leaf out approximately ⅛″ *outside* of the pencil line traced around the pattern (Fig. 3-18).

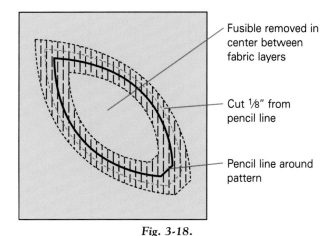

Fusible removed in center between fabric layers

Cut ⅛″ from pencil line

Pencil line around pattern

Fig. 3-18.

3 Remove the paper backing. Turn all the leaves over and fuse them to the back of the teal fabric. Cut each leaf out along the *inside* of the edge of the leaf shape, approximately ⅛″ from the edge. You are cutting on what would be the pencil line around the pattern, although the pencil line doesn't show (Fig. 3-19).

4 Following the pattern for exact placement, attach Leaf 1 and Leaf 2 to the background fabric with a dab of fabric glue: Place the glue along the side of Leaf 1 and the top edge of Leaf 2. Or fuse the leaves in place with a piece of ⅜″ wide paper-backed fusible web tape.

5 To shape the small leaves, first decide which of the two fabrics—the green or the teal—you want to have facing upward. Then place a dab of glue in the center at the base of the leaf on either the right or the wrong side. (Put the glue on the right side if you want the leaves to fold upward; put it on the wrong side if you prefer to have them facing downward.) Gather the leaf fabric by pinching it together, then hold it in place with a clothespin until the glue sets (Fig. 3-20).

6 Set the leaves aside until after you have made the flowers. Since the size and shape of the finished flowers will vary, it is best to tuck the leaves in place after the flowers are attached.

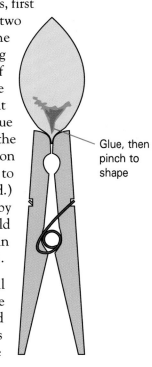

Glue, then pinch to shape

Fig. 3-20.

CRINKLED, HEAT-SET RIBBON ZINNIAS

The two Zinnias in the bouquet are made of crinkled, heat-set ribbon. The Zinnia on the left side is made from a 15″ length of salmon ribbon and 3″ of yellow for the center. The one on the right is made from 12″ of lavender, 10″ of purple, and 3″ of yellow ribbon. To make the Zinnias, work directly on the background fabric, and make one flower at a time.

Fig. 3-19. Left side: *The cut-out appliqué of small leaf template from Figure 3-17. Remove the paper backing.* Right side: *Turn the leaf over and fuse the shape onto the back of the teal fabric. The final cut is made ⅛″ from the inside of the edge of the leaf shape. (The pencil line is not visible through the layers of the two-sided leaf, but the cut will be on this line.) This shape is now the same size as the actual pattern.*

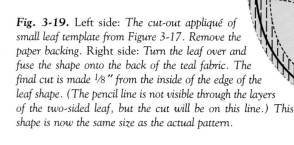

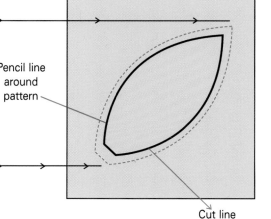

Pencil line around pattern

Cut line

1 First, apply fabric glue to the center of the area on the background fabric where the flower is to go. Attach a small clump of the yellow crinkled, heat-set ribbon in place in the center of the flower.

2 Apply the glue in a spiral direction, about 2″ at a time. Set the ribbon for the outer portions of the flower on top of the glued area, forming the flower as you go (Fig. 3-21). Be sure to push the ribbon closely together to form a dense shape.

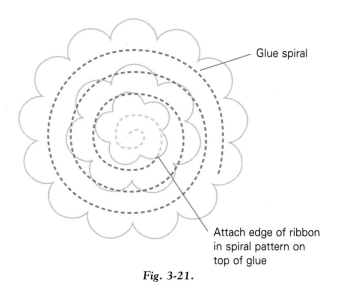

Glue spiral

Attach edge of ribbon in spiral pattern on top of glue

Fig. 3-21.

BOX-PLEATED RIBBON FLOWER

 Like the Zinnias, the Box-Pleated Ribbon Flower is created by working directly on the background fabric. If you can't find ready-made box-pleated ribbon trim, use knife-pleated trim or make your own. (For information on box and knife pleats, see "Pleating" earlier in this chapter.)

1 To make this flower, start with ⅓ yard of box-pleated ribbon trim. Seal the edges with liquid fray preventative.

2 Apply fabric glue to the center of the area on the background fabric where the flower is to go. Place the box-pleated ribbon trim on top of the glued area, then apply the glue in a spiral direction, about 2″ at a time, as you press the edge of the ribbon in place (Fig. 3-21). To give the flower a fuller appearance, condense or gather the ribbon slightly as you

position and press it. (Tweezers are handy for positioning the ribbon.)

3 Cut a 1″ length of thread fringe and glue it in the center to create a cluster of stamens. (I trimmed 1½″ thread fringe down to 1″.)

WIRE-EDGE RIBBON ROSES

 The Roses and Peony in this bouquet are all made from gathered wire-edge ribbon, although slightly different techniques are used. One of the advantages of wire-edge ribbon is that it retains any shape you form it into. It is also very easy to work with, and lends itself to endless variations. The Roses demonstrate how to make wire-edge ribbon flowers by gathering and rolling. (You can gather one wire only or both wires, one tightly and one more loosely.)

1 Cut 18″ of 1″ wire-edge ombre ribbon for each rose. (Use lavender for the rose on the lower left and ruby-red for the one on top of the arrangement.)

2 Apply liquid fray preventative to each end of the ribbon. Pull each wire out about ¼″ and bend it so it will not pull out when you gather the ribbon (Fig. 3-22).

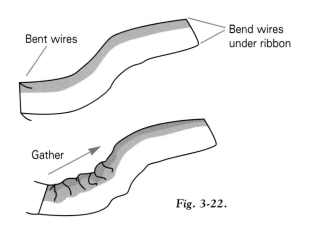

Bent wires

Bend wires under ribbon

Gather

Fig. 3-22.

3 Gather each ribbon to 14″. To do this, hold the bottom wire (D) and pull the ribbon toward the other end, gathering it as you pull to the desired length (Fig. 3-23). As you pull the wire, gather the ribbon into a circle. Take the top corner of the ribbon (B) and fold it down to the bottom edge of the

ribbon, at an angle, toward the inside of the flower; secure it with a dab of fabric glue. Repeat the same step on the other side, angling the corner (A) to either the outside or the inside, depending on where you want it.

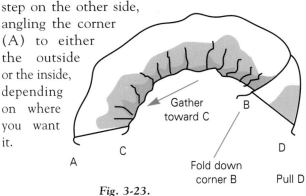

Fig. 3-23.

4 Roll the center part tightly, with the angled end of the flower facing inward (Fig. 3-24). Roll more loosely toward the outer edges so the flower will flair out. Apply fabric glue to the base of the flower, then attach the flower to the background fabric. (I use FabriTac, which bonds quickly.) Another option is to wrap the bottom edge of the finished flower with the wire and then apply fabric glue. The size of the flower is determined by how tightly you wrap the ribbon. The petals can then be folded and shaped, or pushed open. (If you are using ribbon without wire, simply roll and glue the ribbon in place at the base.)

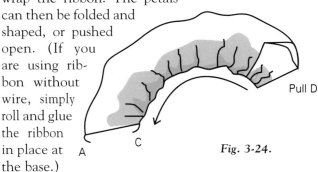

Fig. 3-24.

5 To make a stem for the rose on the left, cut a 7″ length of green cord. Fold it in half, then twist it like a candy cane, four or five times. Apply a line of glue to the background fabric, then secure the twisted cord in place. If necessary, place a weight on the cord until the glue is set.

WIRE-EDGE RIBBON PEONY

The Peony is made using a slightly different technique: Instead of gather-ing and rolling the ribbon from one end to the other, you fold it in half first, then twist in the center so the darker and lighter edges are reversed on different ends.

1 Take 1 yard of 1½″-wide ombre wire-edge rib-bon and apply liquid fray preventative to each end. Pull each wire out about ¼″ and bend it to secure it.

2 Mark the center of the ribbon with a pin. Take the top corner (C) and fold it down on an angle (Fig. 3-25); secure the ribbon in place with a dab of glue. Do the same with the other end (B).

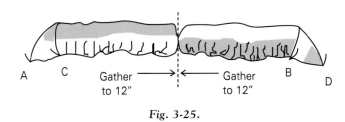

Fig. 3-25.

3 At the center mark, twist the ribbon a half turn until the dark side of the ribbon is on the top on the left side (Fig. 3-25).

4 On the right side of the ribbon, with the dark side on the bottom, gently pull the right bottom wire (D) to gather the ribbon toward the center until that side is 10″ long. On the left side, with the light side on the bottom, gently pull the left bottom wire (A) to gather the ribbon toward the center until that side is 12″ long.

5 Working directly on the background fabric, apply the gathered wire-edge ribbon on top of the glued area (Fig. 3-26). To do this, apply fabric glue in a spiral direction, about 2″ at a time, as you press the edge of the ribbon in place. (FabriTac works well for this purpose, since it bonds in-stantly. You may find tweezers useful for push-ing and pulling the ribbon in place.)

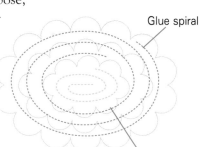

Fig. 3-26.

6 When the wire-edge ribbon is glued in place, cut a 6″ piece of yellow crinkled, heat-set ribbon. Apply a spiral of fabric glue in the center of the flower, then push the yellow ribbon in place.

STRETCHED AND GATHERED JERSEY HOLLYHOCK

To form this flower, use a jersey knit fabric. An old T-shirt or a piece of cotton knit from the remnant section of your fabric store will work fine, as long as it can be stretched out of shape. Just be sure not to use fabric with Lycra in it, because it will return to its original shape.

I started with a white cotton jersey knit and painted it for effect. If you would like to paint the fabric, cut the strip, then wet it thoroughly. Dip a sponge brush into dye (or thinned paint) and dab it along the top and bottom edges of the strip, allowing the color to bleed toward the center. While the fabric is still wet, take a lighter-color dye (or thinned paint) and brush it down the center of the strip. The colors will bleed into one another, and the edges will dry darker, giving a natural look to the flower. Heat-set when dry. (For more information on painting and dying fabric, see Chapters 5 and 6.)

1 To make the Hollyhock, take the 2½″ × 8″ piece of knit fabric and cut the strip *across* the grain (knit), not *along* the grain (selvage).

2 Cut one 1″ piece of yellow crinkled, heat-set ribbon and one 3″ piece of wire thread. (Clear monofilament thread can also be used.)

3 Lay the jersey strip down and gather it together in the center, like a bow tie. Place the yellow crinkled, heat-set ribbon in the center, then wrap the wire thread around the center (Fig. 3-27). Twist

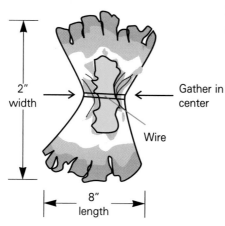

2″ width — Gather in center

Wire

8″ length

Fig. 3-27.

the wire in the back of the flower to secure.

4 Bring the ends of the fabric together to form a circle (Fig. 3-28). Apply glue to the center of the flower, then secure the flower to the background fabric.

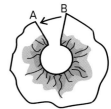

Fig. 3-28.

GATHERED RUFFLE HANGING BELLFLOWER

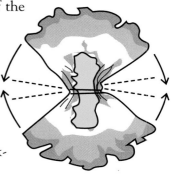

1 Cut 3″ of 1½″ wide gathered ruffle. Apply a dab of glue along the cut end A; overlap the cut end B on top of A (Fig. 3-29). Hold the ends together for a few seconds until the glue sets.

2 For the stamen, cut a 4″ piece of yellow crinkled, heat-set ribbon. Fold it in half or off-center, then push the fold of the stamen into the center of the flower, with the fold protruding through the center approximately ½″.

A　B
Glue A to B
Fig. 3-29.

3 Take a 7″ length of green cord for the stem, and pull it through the center of the stamen until the two sides of the cord are the same length. (Fig. 3-30). Pull the stamen back into the flower until the stem is inside the flower.

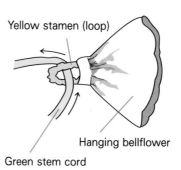

Yellow stamen (loop)

Hanging bellflower

Green stem cord

Fig. 3-30. *Pull the fold (loop) of the stamen through the back of the flower so it protrudes approximately ½″. Insert the green cording through the stamen loop until the two sides of the cording are equal. Then pull the stamen back into the flower.*

4 Apply fabric glue inside the flower, around the stamen and the stem. Pinch the flower shape, along with the stamen, together at the base. Hold for a few seconds until the glue sets. Allow to dry completely.

5 Take 3″ of ⅜″ green grosgrain ribbon for the calyx and seal the ends with liquid fray preventative. Apply a dab of fabric glue to the outside base of the flower, then attach one end of the green ribbon; hold until the glue sets. To form the calyx, wrap the ribbon in a spiral around the outside base of the flower, twisting tighter as you move down to the stem. Apply dabs of fabric glue as you wrap. Hold the calyx in place with a clothespin until dry.

6 Apply fabric glue to the background fabric for the stem and the calyx. (The flower itself is not attached to the background.) Quickly twist the green stem cord several times, in candy-cane fashion, and secure it in place. If necessary, place a weight on top of the cord until the glue sets.

GATHERED POPPY

 This flower is made using fabric stiffener to give it shape. I selected sandwashed rayon, but just about any soft, lightweight fabric will work. When choosing your fabric, consider how much fraying you want, if any. You can even use sheer fabric, as long as it doesn't fray *too* much.

1 Using the templates in Figure 3-31, cut one 3″ circle and one 2½″ circle from the scarlet fabric.

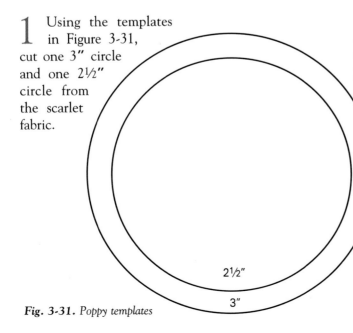

Fig. 3-31. *Poppy templates*

2 To make the stamens, cut a 2″ square out of dark novelty fabric. Fringe the square by making ½″ parallel cuts into each side, then cut out the corners.

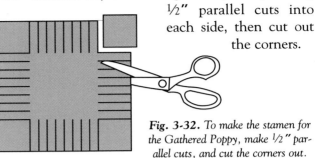

Fig. 3-32. *To make the stamen for the Gathered Poppy, make ½″ parallel cuts, and cut the corners out.*

3 Center the 2½″ circle on the 3″ circle. Then center the stamen fabric on top of both circles (Fig. 3-33). With your index finger or a blunt object, push the center of the two circles and the stamen toward the back, pinching it together in the back. Wrap the pinched fabric with a rubber band, wire thread, or thread to hold it in place.

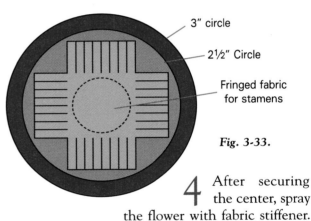

3″ circle

2½″ Circle

Fringed fabric for stamens

Fig. 3-33.

4 After securing the center, spray the flower with fabric stiffener. As it dries, arrange the outer petals and stamens into a shape that you like; once the stiffener dries completely, the flower will retain its shape. Before attaching the flower to the background fabric, remove the rubber band or thread, and cut off any excess fabric. (The stiffener helps hold the center of the flower together and seal the edges of the fabric.) Following the pattern, apply glue directly to the background fabric where the flower is to go, then attach the flower.

FINISHING TOUCHES

The final step in this project is to tuck the leaves in place around the flowers. Position the leaves according to the pattern, or simply tuck them in wherever you like. Attach them with a dab of fabric glue.

Morning Glory Block

This cheerful bird- and morning glory-filled basket demonstrates several ways that pleating, folding, and rolling fabric can add dimension and texture to your projects. On the bird, two styles of pleats are used to represent feathers: sharply pressed pleats on its wing, and softer pleats on its tail. Notice how the interplay of light and shadow adds depth, especially on the deeper, softer pleating on the tail. The vase also illustrates how light and shadow can serve as design elements on pleated shapes. The leaves in the basket demonstrate how you can mold lifelike forms from fabric by simply folding it; the buds and blossom are formed by rolling ribbon, producing a natural effect. Use Figure 3-34 as a guide to the various parts of the block, referred to in the step-by-step directions that follow.

FABRIC AND SUPPLIES

- 13" × 16" dark plum fabric for background fabric
- 9" × 15" cream lining fabric for Pleated Vase
- ¼ yd. multicolored fabric for bird
- 4" × 10" dark green solid fabric for leaves
- 4" × 10" medium green print fabric for leaves
- 5½" × 5½" dark royal blue sheer fabric for Origami Morning Glories
- 5½" × 5½" turquoise metallic lamé for Origami Morning Glories
- Scrap of Ultrasuede for calyxes
- ⅓ yd. of 1½" wide wire-edge ombre ribbon for Rolled Blossom and Buds
- 30" turquoise cording
- 3" trim for Pleated Vase
- ¼ yd. lightweight fusible interfacing for back of pleated fabrics
- ⅓ yd. of ⅜" paper-backed fusible web tape
- ¼ yd. paper-backed fusible web
- Bead, button, or other embellishment for bird's eye
- Scrap of ribbon or fabric for bird's beak and legs
- Fabric glue
- Liquid fray preventative
- Compass
- *Optional:* Paint for spraying the vase

Finished Size. Block: 12" × 15". This is Block B from the *Way-Beyond Baltimore Album Quilt*, which is 38" × 44".

Techniques. Pleating, folding, and rolling fabric, as well as basic no-sew appliqué and dimensional appliqué (described in Chapter 2).

Pattern. Page 123.

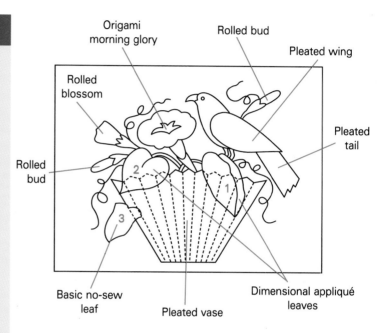

Fig. 3-34. Morning Glory Block

(labels: Origami morning glory; Rolled bud; Pleated wing; Rolled blossom; Pleated tail; Rolled bud; Basic no-sew leaf; Pleated vase; Dimensional appliqué leaves)

PLEATED VASE

1 Cut a 12" × 8" piece of fabric for the vase. Cut a slightly smaller piece of lightweight fusible interfacing. Fuse the interfacing to the back of the vase fabric according to the manufacturer's directions.

2 Make thirteen ¼" pleats in the vase fabric. You can either use a Perfect Pleater or mark the fabric and pleat it by hand (see "Pleating" earlier in this chapter). If you like, you can spray the pleated fabric and the trim for the bottom of the vase with paint for added interest and dimension. (For details on spraying paint on fabric, see Chapter 5.)

3 With the pleated fabric face up, cut along lines A and B on either end of the pleated fabric (Fig. 3-35). Fold the shaded part between pleat 12 and 13 toward the back of the fabric, and press along the fold line. (Use a press cloth to prevent scorching.) The shaded part between pleat 1 and 2 should already be folded toward the back of the fabric.

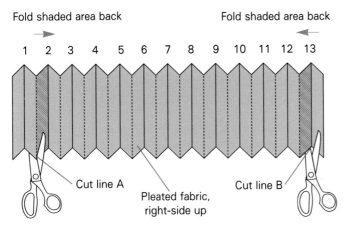

Fig. 3-35.

4 Turn the pleated fabric face down. Fuse ⅜" paper-backed fusible web tape along the two outer edges (Fig. 3-36). Remove the paper backing and fuse these two outer sections to the back of the pleated vase fabric to make finished edges on both sides. To avoid distorting the pleats, be careful to press along the strip only.

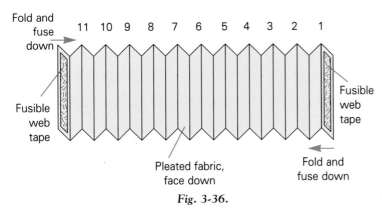

Fig. 3-36.

5 Fold the pleats so the vase fabric lies flat. (If necessary, pin the pleats to keep the fabric flat.) Then place Template V in Figure 3-37 on top of the pleated fabric, pin it in place, and cut the vase out. If necessary, apply liquid fray preventative to the top and bottom edge of the vase.

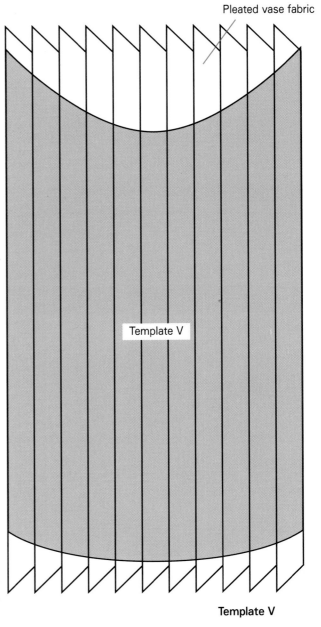

Fig. 3-37. *Vase template on pleated fabric*

6 Fuse a piece of ⅜" paper-backed fusible web tape directly on the background fabric along the bottom inside edge of the vase. Remove the paper backing. Fan out the pleats across the top, and match the sides to fit the pattern. Secure the sides and bottom of the pleated vase fabric with a few pins; glue the sides in place (Fig. 3-38). Next, fuse the vase at the bottom, using a press cloth to prevent scorching. It will take extra time to fuse through the several thicknesses of the pleats. Turn the block over and

press the bottom of the vase from the back to ensure a secure bond.

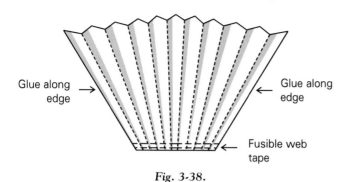

Glue along
edge →

← Glue along
edge

← Fusible web
tape

Fig. 3-38.

BIRD

1 Using basic no-sew appliqué, trace the pattern pieces for the bird's head, beak, and legs onto paper-backed fusible web. (Be sure to reverse the pattern.) Fuse these pieces to the fabric, cut them out, and remove the paper backing. Then fuse them to the background fabric, following the pattern.

2 To pleat the fabric for the tail, cut a 5″ × 6″ piece of fabric. Cut a slightly smaller piece of lightweight fusible interfacing, then fuse the interfacing to the back of the tail fabric according to the manufacturer's directions. Following the steps under "Pleated Vase" above, make four ¼″ pleats. Finish and fuse the sides of the tail the same way you finished the sides of the vase. Use Template T in Figure 3-39 to cut the tail from the pleated fabric. Fuse the top of the tail to the background fabric (it will eventually be underneath the wing) with ⅜″ paper-backed fusible web tape.

3 To form the wing, cut a 3½″ × 18″ piece of fabric. Cut a slightly smaller piece of lightweight fusible interfacing, and fuse it to the back of the wing fabric according to the manufacturer's directions. Make ¼″ pleats the entire length of the fabric. Then trace Template W in Figure 3-39 onto paper-backed fusible web, allowing extra space around the tracing

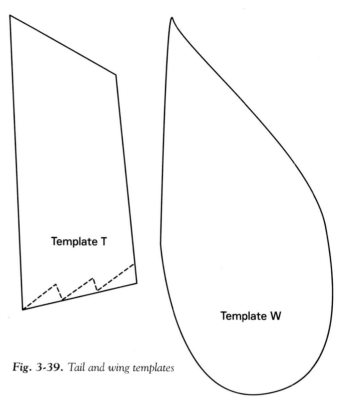

Template T

Template W

Fig. 3-39. Tail and wing templates

line. Check to make sure the pleats are facing the correct direction, then fuse the web to the back of the pleated fabric (Fig. 3-40). Cut out the wing along the traced line, then remove the paper backing and fuse the wing to the background fabric. Use a press cloth to prevent scorching. If necessary, use liquid fray preventative around the wing. Turn the block over and apply heat to the back of the wing to ensure a secure bond.

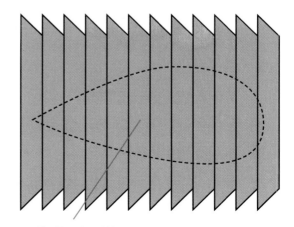

Pin Template W onto pleated fabric and cut out

Fig. 3-40. Wing template on pleated fabric

4 To finish the bird, glue a bead, button, or embellishment in place for the eye.

ORIGAMI MORNING GLORY

Before making the Morning Glory, you will be adding the cording tendrils that twine out of the basket. You may also want to practice making the flower with paper before you begin folding the fabric.

1 Cut the turquoise cording to size and seal the ends with liquid fray preventative. Use fabric glue to apply them to the background fabric according to the pattern.

2 To create the reversible or two-sided fabric for the Origami Morning Glory, cut a 5½″ × 5½″ square of dark royal blue nylon and a slightly smaller piece of lightweight paper-backed fusible web; fuse the two together. Remove the paper and fuse to the back of the 5½″ × 5½″ piece of turquoise metallic lamé. (Always use a press cloth and a no-stick pressing sheet when fusing fine, synthetic, or metallic fabrics.)

3 Mark and cut a 5″ × 5″ square from the two-sided fused fabric and fold it in half horizontally, with the dark side of the fabric inside the folded square. Press, then mark the center on the top and bottom lightly with a pencil, or fold the square in half and finger-press the crease (Fig. 3-41).

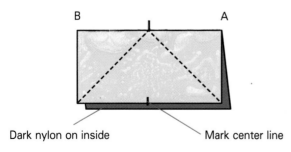

B   A

Dark nylon on inside   Mark center line

Fig. 3-41.

4 Fold corner A toward the front to the center. Turn the form over and fold corner B toward the back to the center (Fig. 3-42). Press flat.

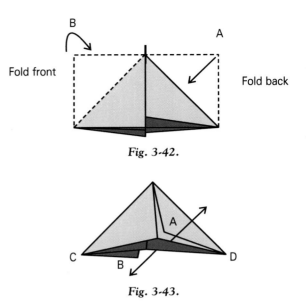

Fold front   Fold back
B   A

Fig. 3-42.

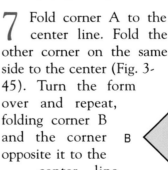

Fig. 3-43.

5 Open up the folded square of fabric and refold so that corners C and D are touching and the figure is again folded flat (Fig. 3-43). Press.

6 Turn the figure upside down so that corners C and D are at the top (Fig. 3-44).

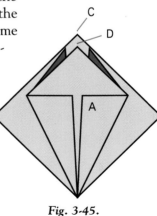

Fig. 3-44.

7 Fold corner A to the center line. Fold the other corner on the same side to the center (Fig. 3-45). Turn the form over and repeat, folding corner B and the corner opposite it to the center line. Press.

Fig. 3-45.

8 Pull corner E out (Fig. 3-46) and fold it about halfway along the inner fold line so it

Fig. 3-46.

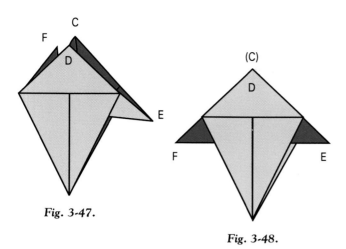

Fig. 3-47.

Fig. 3-48.

1 To make the dimensional appliqué leaves, use Templates 1 and 2 in Figure 3-51. Reverse the designs, trace the leaves (one each of 1 and 2) onto paper-backed fusible web, and cut them out about ¼″ outside the pencil line.

forms a point (Fig. 3-47). Repeat with corner F. The figure should look like Figure 3-48 when you are finished.

9 Using a compass, mark the curve as shown in Figure 3-49. Cut along the curved line with sharp scissors.

Fig. 3-49.

10 Pull the front open to complete the Morning Glory shape (Fig. 3-50). Steam press, using a press cloth to prevent scorching. If necessary, add a few dabs of fabric glue to keep the folds from opening. Hold the flower in place with a clothespin or weight until the glue sets.

11 Apply fabric glue to the back of the Morning Glory. Attach the flower to the background fabric, following the pattern.

Fig. 3-50.

LEAVES

The dimensional appliqué leaves for this project are made from reversible or two-sided fabric. For more details on how to make them, see the directions under "Leaves" for the *Full-Blown Flowers Block* beginning on page 37.

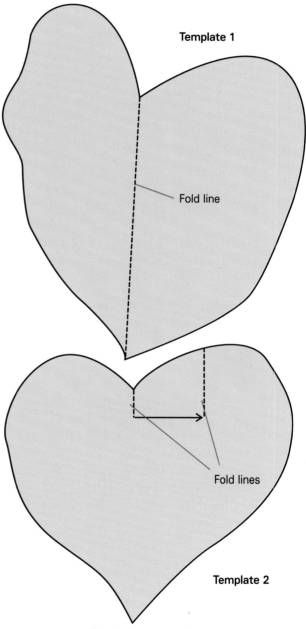

Template 1

Fold line

Fold lines

Template 2

Fig. 3-51. *Leaf templates*

2 Cut out the center of the shapes (cut from fusible web) to make the leaves more flexible. Fuse these shapes to the dark green solid fabric, then cut them out about ⅛″ outside the traced line.

3 Sandwich the cording for the stem between the two fabrics, then fuse each leaf onto the back of the green print fabric.

4 Cut ⅛″ along the inside of the shapes. Each leaf should now be the same size as the actual pattern piece.

5 To add shape to the leaves, fold them as shown in Figure 3-51. Place a dab of fabric glue inside the fold of Leaf 2 to secure it. Press the fold of Leaf 1 with an iron.

6 To make Leaf 3, trace the pattern on page 123. Reverse the pattern, trace it onto paper-backed fusible web, and fuse the web to the back of the printed green fabric. Cut out the leaf, then fuse it onto the background fabric, following the pattern.

7 Attach the leaves to the background fabric with fabric glue.

ROLLED BLOSSOM AND BUDS

I used 1½″ wire-edge ombre ribbon for the buds and blossom, but bias-cut binding or fabric is also a good choice.

1 To make the blossom, remove the top wire from a 6″ piece of 1½″ wire-edge ombre ribbon. Seal the ends with liquid fray preventative. Pull both ends of the bottom wire out about ¼″ and bend them so they will not pull out when you gather the ribbon. Take corners A and B and fold them down to the bottom edge of the ribbon at an angle, toward the inside; secure them with a dab of fabric glue (Fig. 3-52). Gather the ribbon to 3½″ by pulling the remaining wire. Roll the gathered ribbon up loosely, then squeeze the ribbon together at the bottom to form the blossom. Attach to the background fabric with a dab of fabric glue.

2 To make the buds, cut two 3″ pieces of 1½″ wire-edge ombre ribbon. Seal the ends with liq-

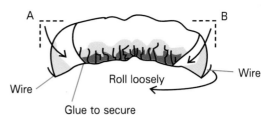

Fig. 3-52.

uid fray preventative. Fold the ribbon as shown in Figure 3-53: First, fold corners A and B toward the bottom edge so they meet in the center, forming a triangle. Then fold C to D, forming a smaller triangle. Hold the top point, then roll the point where C and D meet toward the back. Roll the bud as tight as you like. Apply glue to the bottom of the bud, then attach it to the background fabric.

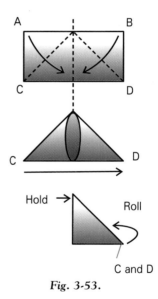

Fig. 3-53.

3 To make the calyxes, trace the pattern pieces for these onto paper-backed fusible web, and fuse to the back of Ultrasuede. Cut out the pieces and fuse them onto the background fabric, covering the base of the flowers and buds. (The calyxes will not fuse flat, so you'll have to work with them.) Glue around some of the forms as needed.

Woven Basket of Flowers Block

Baskets are wonderful shapes and a common motif in quilts. The Woven Basket of Flowers Block illustrates several different weaving techniques that can be used to enrich no-sew appliqué. The basket is made from torn strips of fabric woven in a simple plain weave to add texture and dimension. Woven silk ribbons in mauve and magenta, also in a plain weave, create a checkerboard pattern for the centers of two thistle flowers. A lush mauve pincushion flower is created by weaving strands of threads and ribbons through a looser-weave fabric (Aida cloth). This method leaves loops, resulting in a three-dimensional, tufted flower.

Braiding and coiling are also put to use in this block. The stems are created by braiding three different ribbons together, and coiled cord forms the center of the sunflower, which is made by looping silk ribbon. To complete the composition, knotted fabric is used to create bluebells and a zinnia. Exposed raw edges on these flowers add extra variety and texture. Use Figure 3-54 as a guide to the various parts of the block, referred to in the step-by-step directions that follow.

As you read the directions for this project, keep in mind that the term "thread" can refer to any ribbon, trim, or fabric used for weaving.

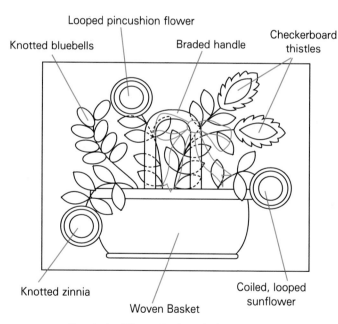

Looped pincushion flower
Knotted bluebells
Braded handle
Checkerboard thistles
Knotted zinnia
Woven Basket
Coiled, looped sunflower

Fig. 3-54. Woven Basket of Flowers Block

Fabric and Supplies list for this project is on the following page

---

Finished Size. Block: 12″ × 15″. This is Block A from the *Way-Beyond Baltimore Album Quilt*, which is 38″ × 44″.

Techniques. Weaving, braiding, knotting, and coiling, as well as basic no-sew appliqué and dimensional appliqué (described in Chapter 2).

Pattern. Page 124.

WOVEN BASKET

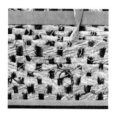

The basket for this block is woven to fit the pattern shape from torn strips of fabric. Since the strips are meant to add texture, you can let them twist and turn at random.

1 Trace the basket pattern on a piece of paper that is several inches larger than the basket shape. About 2″ above and below the edges of the pattern, mark the spacing for the warp (vertical) threads by tracing the pattern or drawing marks at ⅝″ intervals. Tape the pattern on a foamcore board or a piece of corrugated cardboard. Push heavy straight pins through the paper and board (Fig. 3-55). Slant the

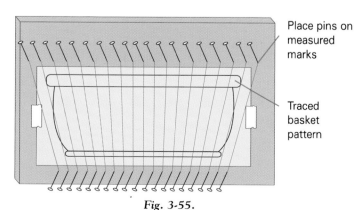

Place pins on measured marks

Traced basket pattern

Fig. 3-55.

FABRIC AND SUPPLIES

13" x 16" dark plum fabric for background fabric

12" x 6" dark plum fabric for warp of Woven Basket

10" x 10" medium brown fabric for weft of Woven Basket

3" x 12" medium color fabric for Braided Handle

Scrap of green fabric for leaves and outside edges of Checkerboard Thistles

⅛ yd. or 8" x 10" piece of Ultrasuede for leaves

1" x 44" strip of multicolored fabric for Knotted Zinnia

8" x 4" strip or scraps of light blue fabric for Knotted Bluebells

8" x 4" strip or scraps of dark blue fabric for Knotted Bluebells

1 yd. each of 3 different 1⁄16" wide ribbon or Ribbon Floss for stems

16 2" pieces of yellow embroidery floss

1 spool metallic Ribbon Floss for Looped Pincushion Flower

1 spool Sulky Sliver metallic thread for Looped Pincushion Flower

1 spool each of 3 other decorative and metallic coordinating threads for Looped Pincushion Flower

5 yds. of 4mm mauve silk ribbon or ⅛" ribbon for Checkerboard Thistles

3 yds. of 4mm magenta silk ribbon or ⅛" ribbon for Checkerboard Thistles

6 yds. of 4mm gold silk ribbon or ⅛" ribbon for Coiled, Looped Sunflower

9" twisted gold cord for Coiled, Looped Sunflower

28" of 1"-wide ribbon for bow

¼ yd. nonwoven lightweight fusible interfacing

2" x 10" piece of brown Ultrasuede for Woven Basket trim

Scrap of Aida cloth (or Vinyl-Aida fabric) for Looped Pincushion Flower

⅛ yd. paper-backed fusible web

Fabric glue

Liquid fray preventative

Upholstery or tapestry needle

Foamcore board or piece of corrugated cardboard

Heavy straight pins

heads of the pins away from the center. (If you are creating your own designs, keep in mind that the proper spacing depends on the tightness of the weave or the thickness of the warp and weft threads; generally ¼" to ½" works well. It is best to have an odd number of warp threads to create a balance on both sides of the weaving.)

2 Tear 19 strips of dark plum fabric for the warp, 6" long and ⅝" wide. To tear, cut slits at one end of the fabric, ⅝" apart, and tear the fabric at each slit. Tear 16 strips of medium brown fabric for the weft, 10" long and ⅝" wide.

3 To set up the warp, place your strips of fabric (or ribbon, trim, or cords) face down. (It is best to weave with the warp and weft facing the board. That way, it's easy to apply fusible interfacing or fusible web to the back of the weaving to increase stability.) Secure each strip with a pin at the top and bottom. As you pin, try to make the tension even. If you like, you can use masking tape over the strips of fabric to hold them in place and to keep the warp threads from fraying or tearing (Fig. 3-56).

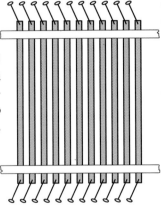

Fig. 3-56.

4 Using your fingers, a tapestry or upholstery needle, or a flat object to lift and push the warp threads, weave with the weft (horizontal thread) right side down in an over-and-under pattern. When you finish a row, pin the ends in place, slanting the pin heads away from the center of the project (Fig. 3-57).

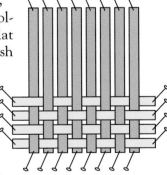

Fig. 3-57.

5 Continue weaving new strips until you have used all 16 strips. (You may need more, depending on the weight of the warp and weft fabric.)

6 When the weaving is completed, place paper-backed fusible web or lightweight fusible interfacing over it. Fuse lightly in place. Remove the pins, then turn the weaving over. Cover the weaving with a press cloth and fuse permanently, following the manufacturer's directions. The woven fabric can now be used the same way as any other fabric.

7 After stabilizing the weaving with interfacing or fusible web, mark and cut out the basket shape. Fuse the basket to the background fabric, following the pattern.

BRAIDED HANDLE

1 Tear or cut three strips of basket fabric, 1″ wide and 12″ long. Tie or tape the three strands together at one end. Secure this end with tape on a work surface, or tie it to something like a doorknob.

2 Work the strands one over the other as shown in Figure 3-58: Alternate placing the outside strand over the center strand, using first the outside right strand, then the outside left, and so forth. Continue until you have a braid about 12″ long. Shake the unbraided strands every few inches so they won't get tangled.

3 Press the braided handle with a hot steam iron if it is too thick.

4 Double-check the length of the handle you need by measuring the braid against the pattern. Then secure the end of the braid by wrapping a piece of tape around it. (Trim the tape off after gluing the handle in place.) Or use a dab of fabric glue just above the spot where you plan to cut the braid, to prevent it from coming apart.

Fig. 3-58.

5 Place a line of fabric glue on the background fabric, following the pattern, and glue the braided handle in place.

LEAVES AND STEMS

1 To make the stems, cut 36″ lengths of three different ¹⁄₁₆″ wide ribbons and braid them together. Use the pattern to determine the lengths of braided stem you need, then secure the ends of the braids with a dab of fabric glue and cut them apart. Place a line of fabric glue on the background fabric, and glue the braided stems in place.

2 To make the leaves, trace 15 leaves onto paper-backed fusible web using the template in Figure 3-59. Be sure to allow enough space around each leaf to cut around it with pinking shears. Fuse the traced leaves onto the back of the leaf fabric, and cut them out with pinking shears. Then fuse them onto the background fabric, following the pattern.

Fig. 3-59.
Leaf template

LOOPED PINCUSHION FLOWER

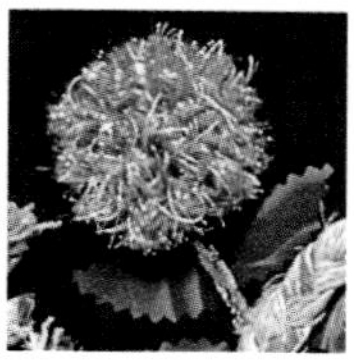

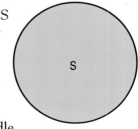

This flower is created with a weaving technique that leaves loops, resulting in a look that resembles punched needlework. Several strands of threads and ribbons are threaded through a tapestry needle and woven together as one unit through vinyl or fabric Aida cloth.

1 Draw around Template S in Figure 3-60 on either vinyl or fabric Aida cloth. Cut out the circle. Seal the edges with liquid fray preventative, if necessary.

2 Thread a tapestry needle with the selected ribbons and threads. (I combined one strand of metallic Ribbon Floss, one strand of Sulky Sliver metallic thread, two strands of Sulky rayon thread, and one strand of Sulky metallic thread.)

Fig. 3-60.
Template S

3 Start in the center, and work on one half of the shape, then the other. Weave in an over-one-under-one pattern, but instead of pulling the thread

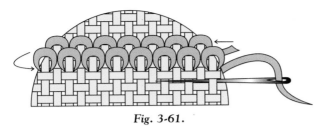

Fig. 3-61.

tight, leave a ½″ loop each time (Fig. 3-61). Continue from side to side.

4 When one-half of the circle is finished, turn the circle and repeat the same process. Don't worry if the loops seem uneven: Just give them a "haircut" when the circle is completely woven.

5 Leave a ½″ "tail" or end of thread on the back. Use fabric glue to adhere the flower to the background fabric. (The "tail" will be secured when the flower is glued down.)

CHECKERBOARD THISTLES

The centers of these flowers are made from a 3″ × 5″ woven piece of "fabric" made from 4mm silk ribbon or ⅛″ ribbon that is framed with an outer edge of leaf fabric.

1 Cut 15 pieces of magenta silk ribbon, each 6″ long, for the warp. On a piece of paper taped to a foamcore board, measure and mark ¼″ intervals for the warp. Pin and tape the ribbon in place, as you did for the basket.

2 Thread mauve silk ribbon through a tapestry and weave it in an over-and-under pattern to create a checkerboard effect. You can cut the ribbon and pin it in place at the end of each row or use a continuous length.

3 Fuse paper-backed fusible web to the back of the ribbon "fabric" to stabilize it.

4 Trace two of Template D1 in Figure 3-62 onto the paper side of the fusible web. Cut out the shapes and fuse them to the background fabric, following the pattern (Fig. 3-63).

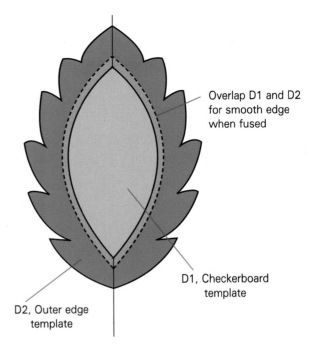

Overlap D1 and D2 for smooth edge when fused

D1, Checkerboard template

D2, Outer edge template

Fig. 3-62. *Checkerboard thistle templates*

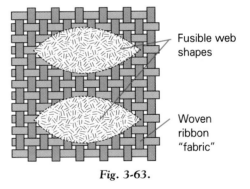

Fusible web shapes

Woven ribbon "fabric"

Fig. 3-63.

5 Trace two of Template D2 in Figure 3-62 onto paper-backed fusible web. Fuse the web to the back of the thistle fabric. Cut around each one, remove the paper, and fuse to the background fabric, following the pattern.

COILED, LOOPED SUNFLOWER

1 Draw around the template in Figure 3-60 on either vinyl or fabric Aida cloth. Cut out the circle. Seal the edges with liquid fray preventative, if necessary. Draw

another circle about ⅛″ inside the outer edge to use as a guide.

2 Thread a tapestry needle with a 24″ piece of 4mm silk ribbon or ⅛″ ribbon. Knot the ribbon at one end. Starting from the back, push the needle through the circle to the front. Pull until the knot is against the back of the circle. To make a series of loops, reinsert the needle *from the back*, next to the first ribbon, but do not pull it tight. Instead, leave a ½″ loop. Repeat this process around the perimeter of the circle (Fig. 3-64). Secure the tails on the back of the circle with a dab of glue.

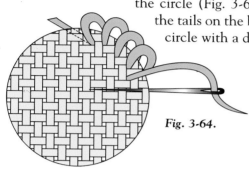

Fig. 3-64.

3 To coil the center of the flower, cut the ends of the gold cord at an angle. Place a dab of glue on the ends and twist lightly to seal. Before gluing the center coil in place, make sure the cord fills the entire center. Apply glue in the center of the front of the looped sunflower. Starting in the center, press one end of the cord down, and slowly turn the piece of Aida cloth, wrapping the cord tightly into a coil (Fig. 3-65). Allow the glue to set.

Fig. 3-65.

4 Apply glue to the back of the Aida cloth. Bond the flower to the background fabric, following the pattern.

KNOTTED ZINNIA AND BLUEBELLS

Although these knotted flowers take only minutes to make, the fabric helps make them look impressive.

To make the overhand knots for either type of flower, simply make a loop in a strip of fabric, and put one of the strip ends through it (Fig. 3-66). Then pull to form the knot. The thickness of the fabric and the tightness of the knot determine the shape of the flower.

Fig. 3-66.

1 The Knotted Zinnia is actually made from a series of knots that are coiled. To make it, tear a 1″ × 44″ strip of multicolored fabric. Make a knot every 2½″ to 3″. (Don't worry about the back or front of the fabric.) Working on a Teflon or nonstick press sheet, start coiling the knotted strip of fabric, gluing as you go. After the glue sets, apply glue to the back of the coiled flower. Bond the flower in place to the background fabric, following the pattern.

2 To make the Knotted Bluebells, tear or cut eight 1″ × 4″ strips each of light and dark blue fabric. Place two strips, one of each color, wrong sides together. Then make an overhand knot, but don't pull it too tight; trim the top or bottom, or both. To make yellow stamens for the bluebells, cut two 2″ pieces of embroidery floss for each flower. Knot each end of the floss, fold both pieces in half, and push them into the center of the knot with a blunt instrument, such as tweezers. Place a dab of glue inside. Glue the individual flowers to the background fabric, following the pattern.

FINISHING TOUCHES

1 Trace the shape for the basket trim from the pattern on page 124. Cut it out from a 2″ × 10″ piece of brown Ultrasuede, then glue the trim in place, following the pattern.

2 Using the template in Figure 3-59, trace eight leaves onto the back of the Ultrasuede. Leave space between the leaves, and cut them out with

pinking shears. Place a dab of fabric glue at the base of each leaf, then bond the leaves to the background fabric, following the pattern.

3 To make the bow, cut a 10″ and an 18″ piece of 1″-wide ribbon. Fold both ends of the 10″ piece toward the center, overlapping 1″ of each end in the center. Secure with a

dab of glue. Lay the 18″ length face down on a flat surface. Take the upper end and wind it as shown in Figure 3-67. Pull the two tails tight to create a knot, then trim the ends. Place a dab of glue in the center of the knot. Bond to the basket handle, following the pattern.

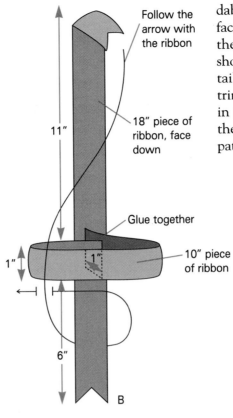

Follow the arrow with the ribbon

18″ piece of ribbon, face down

11″

Glue together

10″ piece of ribbon

1″

1″

6″

B

Fig. 3-67.

CHAPTER 4

EMBELLISHMENTS

Take one look at the textiles of other cultures, and it's easy to see that adorning fabric and clothing with buttons, beads, and ribbons, as well as seashells, charms, and other found objects, is a common design technique the world over. Quilters have always experimented with a variety of surface design techniques, so it's no surprise that they have been inspired by traditional uses of embellishments. The crazy quilts from the late 1800s, for example, incorporated embellishments used on clothing at that time, such as pom-pons and chenille flowers. Today, a surprising array of embellishments appear on contemporary quilts. Innovative new products, such as heat-fusible adhesives, metallic threads and fabrics, and many quick-setting paints, inks, and glues, have had a dramatic impact on the possibilities for embellishing a design.

This chapter provides a wealth of ideas for using a wide variety of embellishments, from ribbons, braids, trims, and threads to beads, sequins, found objects, and appliqués. The simple no-sew techniques presented here can be adapted to almost any type of fabric or style of project.

DESIGNING WITH EMBELLISHMENTS

When adding embellishments to a project, start by asking yourself if they create a separate design or are integrated into the overall design. In other words, are they simply decorative, or do they enhance the design? Embellishments can be used to establish a mood, provide humor, create rhythm, or symbolize a family's heritage. In addition, they can serve to create texture, generate movement, direct the eye with a line, or build a pattern. These adornments can also be used to enrich the colors in a particular piece or to simply add visual interest.

Think of your search for embellishments as a treasure hunt. Spend the time to really look at things and think about unusual ways to use them. Go to antique shops, flea markets, yard sales, and consignment shops for fabrics, buttons, and jewelry. Try hardware stores for doodads. This may be a good time to pull out those old pieces of costume jewelry you saved, or to highlight some of the charms and trinkets that have been collecting dust in a drawer. Who knows? You may finally be able to use those bags of buttons and trims you bought at a close-out sale!

Your search for ideas can be a treasure hunt as well. Investigate other cultures and art forms. Look at old textiles and costumes. Ideas for embellishing, beautifying, adorning, and decorating can come from anywhere, and will add a unique touch to your work.

You can start out simple, if you like. Why not take a piece you already have in progress? You could revive that block you stashed away for a rainy day, and try adding several different embellishments to it. Or jazz up a plain piece of clothing in your closet by decorating it with pieces of lace or appliqué.

USING RIBBONS, BRAIDS, AND TRIMS

Ribbons, braids, and trims provide a wealth of opportunities for adding decorative embellishments to projects. They can be used to add immense variety in shape, texture, color, and sheen. Ribbons come in hundreds of widths, colors, textures, and styles. There are grosgrain ribbons, velvet ribbons, metallic and taffeta ribbons, wire-edge ribbons, and woven-edged ribbons—all with endless uses. Braids, which are made of three or more interwoven strands of fabric or fabriclike material, are especially useful because of their flexibility. Unlike ribbon, braids have a natural give and can be curved and twisted

Tips for Success

EMBELLISHMENTS

Look for embellishments in craft stores and flea markets, as well as your own sewing drawers, jewelry boxes, and junk drawers. Here are some suggestions for using them successfully:

♦ Incorporating embellishments is often a process of experimentation. Arrange them on the surface of your project, then experiment not only with placement, but also with adding and subtracting them. Stay open-minded when working with them.

♦ Don't adhere embellishments until you have an arrangement that pleases you.

♦ Once you have an arrangement you like, make a reference for placement. (It is all too easy to forget how you had the embellishments arranged!) Make a sketch or take a photograph (a Polaroid, if possible) of the layout, or mark the top in some fashion.

♦ Use the proper adhesive for each embellishment. Invest a little time in experimenting before you actually work on your finished piece—It will be worth the time. It's also best to test liquid adhesives on a sample before using them on your work.

♦ Keep in mind that embellishments add weight to your piece, and compensate with the proper backing and batting.

♦ Add embellishments after you have quilted and added the binding to your piece.

♦ To add embellishments to clothing, prewash the fabric before adding the embellishments. Once they have been added, hand wash the clothing with care.

♦ For quilts with embellishments, spray with a fabric protectant first. To clean them, brush with a feather duster, tie a nylon stocking over the vacuum cleaner hose and vacuum, or place a fine mesh or screen over the surface and vacuum lightly through it.

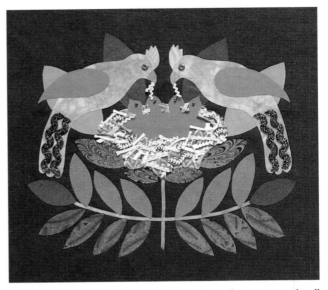

Bird Nest Block. *Ordinary ribbons, braids, and trims can make all the difference in a project if they are used creatively. This whimsical block features a nest constructed of scraps of trim. Rickrack worms nourish the hungry babies; ribbon branches support the nest.*

Bird Nest Block Materials. *A mixture of trims, cut to varying lengths and allowed to fray, take on an entirely different texture when they are clustered into a nest shape and fastened down with fabric glue.*

easily. You can use them to add free-form lines or to outline curves in a project. There are many kinds of trims as well, from ordinary rickrack to an array of decorative cords, tassels, and iron-ons. Trims are available in a multitude of textures, widths, and patterns, and they come in solid as well as variegated colors.

All these materials can be used for more than just decoration. For example, ribbons, braids, and trims are useful for outlining a shape or drawing a line to accentuate a design. They can become loops, tassels, and fringe, and can even provide a finished edge or border for a piece. The bird's nest in the *Bird Nest Block*, created from various trims cut in short lengths, illustrates how these materials can be used to represent a particular object. In Chapter 3, we explored some of the possibilities for pleating and gathering ribbon to make a variety of flowers.

Fortunately, ribbons, braids, and trims are all very easy to use. For best results, seal the edges with liquid fray preventative. (Or, if you prefer, you can use the frayed ends for added texture and visual interest.) Fusible web tape is useful when attaching some ribbons, braids, and trims.

DECORATING WITH THREADS

These days, thread is much more than ordinary sewing thread. An interesting, diverse assortment of threads is available from fabric stores and craft shops everywhere. Choices range from fancy ornamental metallics and silks to ribbon threads, rayon threads, woolly nylon threads, novelty threads, embroidery floss, and nubby and variegated yarns. These can be used as embellishments in a variety of ways to create color, texture, line, and various visual effects, such as movement.

Any combination of threads can be used as embellishment. Bunched or twisted together, threads can look entirely different than if used individually. Try different combinations—There are no rules to follow, so have fun experimenting! See what effects you can create by mixing various colors, weights, and types of threads in a project. Note how the coils and twists of different threads interact with the background, producing an illusion of movement and pattern. You can also create a range of textures, from soft and fluffy to shiny and sharply defined. The *Galaxy Wall Quilt* illustrates some of the effects that are possible with thread.

When you combine threads, secure the ends with liquid fray preventative, or wrap transparent tape around them to prevent raveling. When you cut threads that could ravel, place transparent tape around them and cut through the center.

Galaxy Wall Quilt. *Various types and textures of threads flow across the surface of this quilt, echoing the movement of the pattern and adding visual interest, texture, and dimension. This piece also combines shiny and matte threads to produce a shimmering effect.*

Galaxy Wall Quilt. *An additional layer of embellishments adds even more excitement to this quilt. Pinwheels of clustered beads imitate the movement of the pattern, while star sequins and beads glitter like stars in the night sky.*

USING BUTTONS, BEADS, AND SEQUINS

We often think of these embellishments as either shiny and gaudy or purely functional. However, buttons, beads, and sequins come in hundreds of shapes, sizes, and colors. There are brass buttons and shell buttons, round and square buttons. Beads come in various forms, too, including tiny glass beads, oblong bugle beads, and large wooden beads. You can even paint or dye seeds and use them as beads. Types of sequins range from simple stars or ovals to large paillettes and iron-on sequins. All provide a variety of opportunities for use as embellishments.

Consider grouping buttons, beads, or sequins together to emphasize a design or a seam. Or use them to "draw" a line or outline a shape, by fastening them down in clusters with adhesive. (You can also string sequins or beads and use them this way.) Try clustering similar buttons, beads, or sequins together to provide color or to represent a shape—for example, flowers made of buttons, with ribbon or trim for the stems and leaves. Or make a distinctive pattern by placing any of these embellishments close together. (For best results, keep in mind the direction they are placed.)

In addition to providing a textural effect and visual interest, buttons can also serve a function. Consider using them to tack or tie layers of fabric together. Or simply add beads or sequins as decorative additions when knotting or tying a quilt. You can also secure buttons and beads with decorative threads cascading from the centers. Be sure to take the added weight of these embellishments into account when you plan binding and backing for a piece.

Buttons, beads, and sequins tend to bring a certain richness to a piece, catching the viewer's eye. They form a natural focal point and can dominate a design, since they often catch and reflect light. Place these embellishments carefully: If they are positioned haphazardly or sparsely, the viewer will have difficulty focusing, and the design won't have the same impact.

To attach buttons, beads, and sequins, apply dabs of glue to the fabric and use tweezers to position the embellishments on top of the glue. If they are fairly large, you can dab fabric glue on the back, or use a plastic button fastener. To attach smaller embellishments like seed beads and sequins, paint fabric glue onto the fabric, then spread out the embellishment; when the glue is dry, lift the piece over a box to collect all the beads that are still loose. You can add sequins individually or by the yard, or you can iron them on. When overlapped, they can provide a snakeskin-type effect.

ADDING CHARMS AND FOUND OBJECTS

The number of embellishments in this category is infinite. Today, charms and trinkets of all kinds can be found in many fabric and quilt shops, as well as consignment and antique shops. "Found objects" can be any objects or materials that have been picked up by chance or faithfully collected and then incorporated into a work of art. Seashells, pebbles, feathers, family trinkets, and old handkerchiefs can all be used in your work, as can curtain rings, washers, nuts and bolts, the colorful strands of wire inside cables, and other hardware. All of these have become familiar

CHARMS AND FOUND OBJECTS BLOCK

Charms and found objects add loads of appeal to this block, which is part of the *Crazy Quilt Fabric Diary*. The block itself is easy to make with basic no-sew appliqué and scraps of fabric. If you look closely, you will find seashells, golden sun and moon charms, an antique velvet leaf, and even metal washers from the hardware store. The bird stamping was painted with Paint it Pretty, a paint designed especially for painting metal. Objects are used alone or to create a variety of patterns, and the result is a piece with fascinating detail, texture, and mood. You will find a guide to the embellishments on this block, as well as directions for making the *Crazy Quilt Fabric Diary*, in Chapter 7

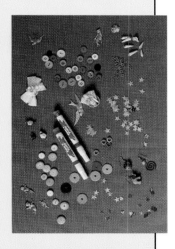

items for decorating quilts and clothing, and can be used to provide visual interest, inject a bit of humor, or add a personal touch to a project.

You'll find charms and found objects everywhere you look. Spend a rainy afternoon rummaging through your old jewelry box, your sewing supplies and notions, or that junk drawer you've been meaning to clean out—You will discover hidden treasures just waiting to be used! Take various objects such as buttons, bows, wire, old jewelry, plastic flowers, dollhouse items, and premade fabric yoyos, and mix them to create a collaged effect. Experiment with a group of items like ties or belts to find new ways of using them as embellishments. Or pull out a pair of your daughter's lacy baby socks or Grandma's favorite handkerchief, and create a fabric collage out of memorabilia.

You can also paint charms and found objects, if you like. Use acrylic jewelry pens that are specifically designed for painting metal embellishments and other items like beads and plastics.

When attaching any of these embellishments, use adhesives that have been specially developed for the materials they are made of. Or wrap and tie them in place with decorative threads. Also, be sure to consider the weight these items add to a piece, and balance with a heavier batting and backing fabric.

USING LACES, LINENS, AND APPLIQUÉS

Laces, linens, and appliqués offer quick and easy ways to transform ordinary clothing, quilts, and home furnishings into something extraordinary. You can use old and new linens, doilies, and handkerchiefs as a substitute for fancy embroidery. Appliqués are useful for embellishing almost anything you can think of, too. The premade appliqués available at fabric stores or quilt shops feature a variety of floral themes, animals, and holiday motifs, as well as monogrammed letters and current popular images such as hearts and stars. However, you don't need to limit yourself to these designs. By using paper-backed heat-fusible adhesives, you can turn almost any shape into a custom-made appliqué. Upholstery and decorator fabrics provide an abundance of motifs, shapes, and designs, such as paisleys, fruits, flowers, birds, and cherubs. (For more ideas on creating your own appliqués from existing images in fabric, see "Broderie Perse" in Chapter 2.)

There are countless ways to create color, pattern, and texture with these embellishments. For example, you can cut motifs, medallions, or scallops from scraps of lace or from embroidered designs and use each element as an individual appliqué. You can also stamp motifs on fabric using some of the techniques described in Chapter 5. In addition, letters, numbers, and pictorial designs can be quickly made into appliqués using fusibles.

When working with laces, linens, and appliqués, choose background fabrics that showcase the embellishments. Contrasting fabric can be a very effective

LACES, LINENS, AND APPLIQUÉS BLOCK

A variety of purchased and custom-made appliqués were chosen for this block from the *Crazy Quilt Fabric Diary.* It's easy to see how these techniques are useful for capturing a mood or creating a cherished remembrance. Here, custom appliqués are made from scraps of lace and other materials. (The chicken is actually an image cut from a piece of fabric.) Purchased appliqués include Ultrasuede hearts and Hershey Kisses. Old embroidered linens are incorporated in the block as well. You will find a guide to these embellishments, as well as directions for making the entire *Crazy Quilt Fabric Diary,* in Chapter 7.

backdrop for delicate fabrics and intricate laces. To prevent damage to antique fabrics, cover them with tulle or netting.

Bird Nest Block

The Bird Nest Block demonstrates a variety of ways to use ribbons, braids, and trims as embellishments. The natural-looking nest, which sits on branches made from thin ribbons, is created by cutting various widths, styles, and colors of these embellishments into confetti and then mixing them together. The baby birds are being fed worms made from narrow rickrack, which adds a touch of whimsy. Wide metallic rickrack adds visual interest and sparkle to both parent birds' tails, and their crests—cut from moiré-patterned ribbon—add sheen and elegance.

FABRIC AND SUPPLIES

13" × 16" dark plum fabric for background fabric

⅛ yd. or scraps of dark solid green for leaves

⅛ yd. or scraps of medium solid teal for leaves

⅛ yd. or scraps of light teal fabric for leaves

⅛ yd. or scraps of 2 different medium prints for leaves

⅛ yd. or scraps of light blue for birds

⅛ yd. or scraps of periwinkle-blue for birds

½ yd. 4mm silk ribbon or ⅛" ribbon for branches

Miscellaneous ribbons, braids, and trims for nest

Scrap of brown fabric for nest

Wide metallic rickrack for bird tails

Scraps of burnt orange and brown moiré ribbon for bird crests and beaks

Narrow rickrack for worms

6 beads or other embellishments for the eyes

¼ yd. paper-backed fusible web

Fabric glue

Liquid fray preventative

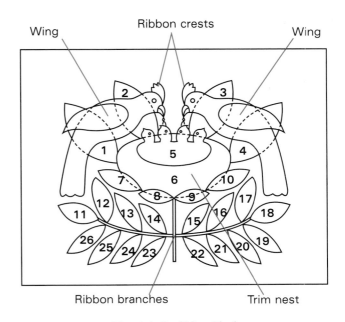

Fig. 4-1. Bird Nest Block

Finished Size. Block: 12" × 15". This is Block C from the *Way-Beyond Baltimore Album Quilt*, which is 38" × 44".

Techniques. Embellishing with ribbons, braids, and trims, as well as basic no-sew appliqué (described in Chapter 2).

Pattern. Page 125.

MAKING THE BLOCK

1 Seal the ends of the ribbons for the branches with liquid fray preventative. Apply a line of fabric glue to the back of the ribbons and position them on the background fabric, following the pattern. Then press the ribbons to bond them to the background fabric.

2 Using basic no-sew appliqué, trace all the appliqué shapes onto paper-backed fusible web. (You do not need to reverse this pattern, since it is a symmetrical design.) Be sure to leave room around each shape. Number the pieces according to the pattern or Figure 4-1; the birds are not numbered and will be added last. Rough-cut the pieces out.

3 Fuse the paper-backed fusible shapes onto the back of the selected fabrics—the leaves from the green fabrics, the birds from the blue fabric, and so forth. Fuse the shapes for the crests and beaks onto a scrap of ribbon. Fuse the shape for the nest onto a brown fabric of your choice. (I used a fabric with a textural pattern to add more dimension.) Cut out the shapes.

4 Following the pattern and the numerical order of the shapes, fuse the appliqué shapes for the leaves, baby birds, and nest onto the background fabric: Fuse the leaves behind the nest first, then the baby birds and the background shape for the nest. Fuse the rest of the leaves last.

5 Position the crests and beaks on the background fabric, then add the birds' bodies and fuse them in place. Add the wings last.

ADDING THE EMBELLISHMENTS

1 Cut the assorted ribbons, braids, and trims you plan to use for the nest into varying lengths, from ¼" to 1". (There is no need to apply fray preventative, since fraying will add to the effect.) Place

a dab of fabric glue on the center of each piece, then place them randomly on top of the bird nest appliqué.

2 Measure and cut pieces of decorative trim to size for the tails. Seal the ends with liquid fray preventative, then bond in place.

3 Cut two pieces of decorative trim (I used narrow rickrack), and glue them in the birds' beaks.

4 Glue beads in place for the eyes, or use a fabric pen to draw eyes.

MORE IDEAS USING RIBBONS, BRAIDS, AND TRIMS

Ribbons, braids, and trims are especially easy to use, since they already have finished edges. Here are some other ideas:

♦ Fuse different widths of ribbons, braids, or trims, or a combination of these, onto a piece of fusible woven interfacing to create a pattern.

♦ Create your own braid from ribbons and trims of the same width.

♦ Create fancy flowers with small pieces of wire-edge or pinked-edged ribbons.

♦ Weave various styles and widths of ribbons, braids, and trims.

♦ Twist and curl ribbons, then spray with a stiffening agent for dimensional effects.

♦ Tear fabric into ribbons, leaving frayed edges, and use them like fringe.

♦ Use a rambling or free-form pattern of ribbons, braids, and trims to form a winding and turning design. Tack them down with fabric glue as you go.

♦ Replace bias binding with ribbons or braids in stained glass appliqué.

♦ Make ribbon flowers to use as embellishments.

Galaxy Wall Quilt

The Galaxy Wall Quilt is made from a traditional pattern that has many names, including Snail's Trail, Monkey Wrench, Virginia Reel, and Indiana Puzzle. All 16 blocks in this quilt are machine pieced and constructed exactly the same way. Although the blocks are relatively simple to make, the clever use of color makes the pattern of the squares and triangles appear very complex. Dark, medium, and light fabrics form an intricate overall pattern that gives the illusion of movement.

This exciting design demonstrates how you can use threads to create a secondary pattern, provide rhythm, and add line to a project. The quilt also features a second level of embellishment: Buttons, beads, and sequins are used to provide even more visual interest. If you look closely, you can see how they echo the pattern and add rhythm and movement to the design. The beads are also used in solid blocks shaped like the quilt pattern, thus adding another level of color and texture.

FABRIC AND SUPPLIES

⅔ yd. dark blue print fabric

⅔ yd. medium blue print fabric

1½ yds. light blue fabric (scrunch dyed)

50″ × 50″ piece of batting

3⅛ yds. backing

1½ yds. light blue fabric for border and binding

Various types and widths of threads for embellishing

Various buttons, beads, and sequins for embellishing (for example, decorative buttons, no-hole glass beads, seed beads, star-shaped beads, and various sizes of star sequins)

Fabric glue

Liquid fray preventative

Bead adhesive

Gem glue

Button fasteners

Rotary cutter

Paintbrush for glue

Finished Size. Wall quilt: 48″ × 48″; individual blocks: 8″ × 8″.

Techniques. Embellishing with threads, buttons, beads, and sequins, as well as scrunch dyeing, color washing, and overdyeing (described in Chapter 6).

SELECTING AND PREPARING FABRIC

Since the focus of this quilt is the galaxy, allow the theme to dictate your fabric choices. I selected a celestial-looking fabric for the darkest color, a fabric with a swirling movement for the medium color, and a scrunch-dyed sky fabric for the lightest color. I positioned the border fabric carefully to blend with the blocks.

Try to construct all the blocks at one time. (I have found that when I sew blocks together at different times, they tend to vary in size, even though they all technically have ¼″ seams. This can present a problem when constructing the quilt, since the seams don't always match as well.) Also, it's a good idea to construct a sample block first, so you can test it and work out any problems. Use the sample block as a sample, then sew all your blocks in a production line.

MAKING THE BLOCKS

Before you begin, wash and press all your fabric. Cut your pieces (with a rotary cutter, if possible) following the cutting chart on the following page. All measurements include a ¼″ seam allowance.

CUTTING CHART

PATTERN PIECE & MEASUREMENT	QUANTITY & FABRIC		
	DARK FABRIC	MEDIUM FABRIC	LIGHT FABRIC
Piece A 1½" square	16	16	32
Piece B 2" square cut across the diagonal to form triangles	8 squares 16 triangles	8 squares 16 triangles	16 squares 32 triangles
Piece C 2½" square cut across the diagonal to form triangles	8 squares 16 triangles	8 squares 16 triangles	16 squares 32 triangles
Piece D 3½" square cut across the diagonal to form triangles	8 squares 16 triangles	8 squares 16 triangles	16 squares 32 triangles
Piece E 4½" square cut across the diagonal to form triangles	8 squares 16 triangles	8 squares 16 triangles	16 squares 32 triangles

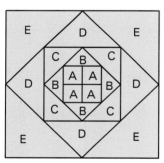

Fig. 4-2. Galaxy Wall Quilt Block

Follow the steps below to make all 16 blocks for the quilt. All are made with the same color pattern, shown in the illustrations. Use Figure 4-2 as a guide to the pattern pieces and their placement. The block construction begins with the center unit, which consists of four patches. Use ¼" seams throughout.

1 Sew one dark and one light A square together. Then sew one medium and one light A square together. Sew these two units together, right sides together, with the light squares opposite

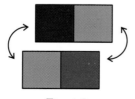

Fig. 4-3.

each other to form a four-patch, as shown in Figure 4-3. Press the seams toward the darker side of the seam so they will not show through.

2 Join size B triangles to the central four-patch, as shown in Figure 4-4. Sew the light fabrics on opposite ends, then add the medium and dark ones so that the dark triangle matches up with the dark square, and the medium triangle with the medium square. Press the seams toward the darker side of the seam.

3 Add size C triangles, as shown in Figure 4-5. Sew the light triangles on opposite ends. Sew the size C dark triangle onto the same side as the size B dark triangle. Match up the medium fabric sizes B and C triangles as well. Press the seams toward the darker side of the seam.

4 Add size D triangles, as shown in Figure 4-6. Follow the same pattern described in Step 3. Press the seams toward the darker side of the seam.

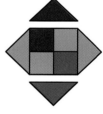

Fig. 4-4.

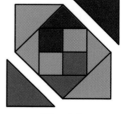

Fig. 4-5.

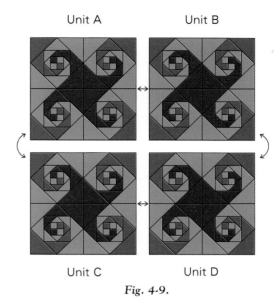

Unit A   Unit B

Unit C   Unit D

Fig. 4-9.

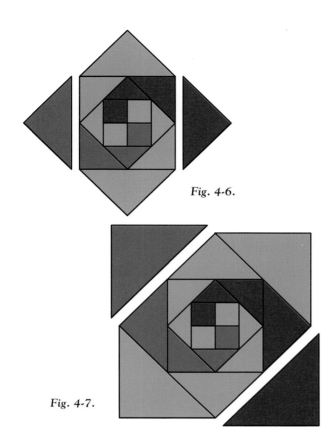

Fig. 4-6.

Fig. 4-7.

Unit B, and Unit C to Unit D. Then sew across the center to join the two sides together.

3 To add the border, cut two 7″ × 50″ strips and two 7″ × 36″ strips from your light blue binding fabric. Sew the two 36″-long strips onto the top and bottom of the quilt. Then sew the two 50″ strips along either side (Fig. 4-10).

5 Finish the block by adding size E triangles, as shown in Figure 4-7. Again, follow the same pattern described in Step 3. Press the seams toward the darker side of the seam.

ASSEMBLING **THE QUILT**

1 To create the pattern, you need to join four blocks together. Turn each block a quarter turn from the one before it, so that all the dark size E triangles meet in the center, and the medium fabric size E triangles form the outer corners (Fig. 4-8).

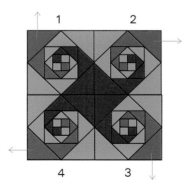

Fig. 4-8.

2 Using ¼″ seams, sew four sets of four blocks together, as shown in Figure 4-9. Sew unit A to

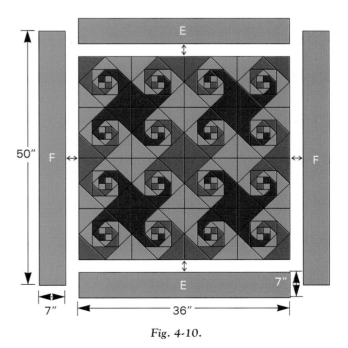

Fig. 4-10.

Fig. 4-11.

4 Mark the top for quilting, as shown in Figure 4-11.

5 Layer the backing, batting, and top. Baste or pin the layers together with safety pins. Then hand or machine quilt. (Be sure to remove the pins as you go.) You will add the thread embellishments and bind the quilt after quilting it.

ADDING THE EMBELLISHMENTS

The thread streamers that flow across the surface of this quilt combine different textures, weights, and shades of threads. See Figure 4-12 for the layout I used, but feel free to come up with your own design: Group threads, or use them in single strands. Make streamers of twisted threads. Combine metallic and novelty threads. Try twisting, turning, wrapping, knotting, and tying them. You can even tie twists of threads in knots, cut them apart, and secure them to the quilt to create small bursts of color. Experiment with laying the thread combinations you have created on top of the quilt, too.

1 After you have determined the design for the threads, spot glue them in place with fabric glue. Space the dots of glue approximately ¼" to ½" apart, depending on the weight of the threads.

2 To bind the quilt, cut four 2"-wide × 54"-long pieces of fabric along the straight of the grain. Sew them together to make lengths for continuous

binding. (For complete instructions on binding, see Chapter 7.) I cut the binding from scrunch-dyed fabric. For details on this technique see "Scrunch Dyeing" in Chapter 6.

3 Attach decorative buttons, beads, and sequins of your choice. See Figure 4-12 for the pattern I used, but, again, feel free to come up with your own design. Use the following techniques to attach the embellishments:

Single-hole beads. Attach variegated single-hole beads by knotting iridescent thread and running it through the bead from the top to the back of the quilt; knot the thread in the back. If the thread frays, apply a bead of glue to secure it.

Other beads. I attached various bugle beads, no-hole glass beads, and other decorative beads to the quilt surface in patterns. To attach these types of beads, paint glue on the quilt with a paintbrush, place the beads thickly on top of the wet glue, then press them in place. After the glue is dry, lift the quilt up and allow the excess beads to fall into a box. When attaching different types of beads within a small area, add one color and style of bead at a time to prevent them from mixing together.

Buttons. Thread large buttons with iridescent thread, and allow them to dangle freely. Then attach the button to the quilt with a button fastener. Secure smaller buttons with fabric glue.

Sequins. Apply a dab of glue to the spot where the sequin is to go. Then place the sequin on top of the glue with tweezers.

Fig. 4-12.

CHAPTER 5

USING PAINT AND INK

Paint and ink are invaluable for creating colorful designs and patterns on fabric. Both can be applied to fabric in more ways than you can imagine—for example, with sponge applicators, foam brushes, squeeze bottles, and mist sprayers, to name just a few. Paint and ink can also be used to print, stamp, or stencil fabric. Paint can be spattered with a stiff brush or even suspended on top of a gelatinous liquid and literally floated onto fabric. Inks are useful for drawing, and can be transferred from a photo to fabric.

This chapter explores a variety of simple, yet versatile techniques for applying paint and ink to fabric. You will find design ideas and projects that use painting, marbling, printing, spraying and spattering, sponging, stenciling and stamping, and even image transfer. You'll also find tips on using fabric pens and textile markers to embellish your projects. Some of the techniques, like block printing, are traditional; others are more contemporary.

There are many paint and ink products on the market—not to mention pens, markers, materials for printing and stamping, spraying supplies, and image transfer materials! To help you sort through all of your options, I have included a list of the products I commonly use, along with suggestions for their use, on page 128.

Before you begin using the techniques described in the following pages, it's helpful to understand a few fundamental differences between paint, ink, and dye. First, paint and ink sit on the surface of the fabric, while dye penetrates it and becomes part of the fibers. For this reason, fabric that has paint or ink on it has a somewhat stiffer feel than dyed fabric. This also explains why painted fabric can be difficult to sew through. (Try to avoid designing a piece that requires sewing any area of fabric that has been painted.)

EXPERIMENT WITH PAINT AND INK

Here's an easy way to learn about all the techniques in this chapter: Buy six or eight solid-color cotton napkins; wash and iron them. Then pick a single motif—for example, an oak leaf, a heart, or a star. Experiment with a different technique on each napkin. For example, stamp your chosen motif on one, paint or stencil it on another. Try repeating the pattern on yet another napkin. You'll find this is a great way to learn how to do the techniques without spending a lot of time, *and* you will have a fun, creative project that you can use at home or give as a gift!

Another important difference is that paint and ink tend to produce bolder colors, with harder, more defined edges than dyes. Because dyes have a transparent quality, they create a more subtle look, with more depth to the color. However, dyes can produce runoff and can stain the surrounding fabric—a problem you won't encounter if you use paint. (For more information on using dyes, see Chapter 6.)

PAINTING TECHNIQUES

Fabric painting is a straightforward process: The paint is simply applied directly to the fabric. Painting fabric can be as carefully planned and detailed—or as spontaneous and abstract—as you want it to be. You can use this technique to create an abstract pattern of color and shape in a watercolor style, for example, or to draw hard lines or even letters on a project. Paint can also be used to make a background design

Southwest Vest. *Three different fabric painting techniques are used to create this vest. The main body of the vest is made with the watercolor technique. Light-sensitive paint is used to create the patterning on the lapels and binding. The pattern on the lining shows the effects of salt crystals.*

that you plan to embellish with trims, ribbons, buttons, or beads. Or you can simply paint a pattern or a pictorial image. The *Southwest Vest* features a variety of painting techniques, including watercolor-style painting, which is used to create stripes of soft, flowing color across the fabric.

Painting How-To

Whatever technique you choose for painting fabric, here are some helpful tips to keep in mind:

Know your fabric—and your product. Read the manufacturer's directions when deciding which product to use. Match the kind of paint to the fabric as well as the technique. There is a paint available for almost any fabric; however, each paint does *not* work equally well on all fabrics. Remember that paints can be thinned or thickened, depending on the technique: Thin paint for spraying and airbrushing; thicken for stenciling, stamping, printing, and sponging.

Always wash fabrics first. Before you start your project, be sure to wash your fabrics to remove any sizing.

Test a sample. Keep in mind that fabric paints *do not* work on materials that have been treated with a repellent finish, such as soil-resistant, crease-resistant, or permanent-press fabrics.

Be prepared. Have everything ready before you start to paint. Be sure to have enough paint prepared, since it is nearly impossible to match a color. Remember: The thicker the fabric, the more paint it will absorb.

Try working in sections. You may want to paint a project in sections, then piece it together when the painting is finished, in case of mistakes.

Experiment with color. Paints can be easily mixed together to create an endless assortment of colors, so don't be afraid to experiment. Also, try layering colors to create depth: Start with a pale color, allow the paint to dry, then add another color on top of it. Keep in mind that the color of the fabric affects the color of the paint. For instance, painting a light color on dark fabric is more difficult than painting a dark color on light fabric. When painting on dark fabric, use opaque colors. Some brands of paint require adding opaque white to make them more opaque, which also makes them paler. Use transparent paints for overlapping and layering motifs. Airbrush inks are very opaque, but thinner than other paint.

Experiment with different effects. Fabric can be wet or dry when you paint it, depending on the technique and the desired effect. If you create an effect that you like while the fabric is still wet, dry it quickly with a hair dryer to keep the paint from blending more. Color that is still wet will dry lighter.

Dry paints properly. Most fabric paints require heat setting; some will air cure. Read the manufacturer's instructions for the product you are using. For best results, allow the paint to cure for several days before washing.

Watercolor Painting

Watercolor painting on fabric is quite similar to traditional watercolor painting on paper. This technique is done on wet fabric; when the brush touches the fabric, the paint immediately spreads, blending and intermingling with other colors. By altering the variables, you can easily achieve a variety of special effects. For example, try spraying the fabric with water, then dripping paint onto the wet fabric. Or paint one color next to another while the first color is still wet, allowing the two to blend. The colors that merge together often create unexpected shades and colors. This technique also yields soft edges and delicate transitions between colors. Once the fabric is dry, you can overpaint with additional colors without having to worry about the colors running into each other.

The watercolor technique can be very effective for a background fabric. (The *Southwest Vest* is a good example.) The type of fabric has some effect on how much the paint flows. Thin, smooth fabric, such as a fine batiste, permits it to flow faster. Paint does not flow as freely on heavier, more textured fabric, such as the silk noil (raw silk) used to make the *Southwest Vest*. A heavier fabric also absorbs more paint.

When using this method, always wash the fabric first. Then stretch it on canvas paint stretchers or an embroidery hoop, or tape it on a work surface padded with newspaper and plain paper. (Use brown paper or unprinted newsprint, available from art supply stores.) Always wet the fabric before painting; you can spray, brush, or sponge it. Thin the paint with water until it has reached the desired color and consistency. Then, using a wide brush, paint across the stretched fabric quickly and evenly from side to side. (Press harder on the brush when working with thicker fabric.) Do *not* stop in the middle of the fabric, or you will make a mark. Allow the paint to dry, then heat-set according to the manufacturer's directions.

Salt Crystal Effects

This easy technique can create truly dramatic effects. Although the results are somewhat difficult to control, they are almost always spectacular! All you have to do is put salt crystals on painted fabric while it is still wet. (You can scatter the crystals, or place them carefully, whichever you prefer.) The salt attracts the moisture in the paint, pulling the paint in various directions. As the crystals absorb the paint from the fabric, a light area with one dark spot under each crystal is formed, creating a sort of starburst effect. Silk tends to be the best fabric for this technique, but cotton works well, too.

To use salt crystals in your project, first wash,

stretch, and moisten the fabric as you would for watercolor painting. Then paint the fabric with the pattern or design desired. (You can draw or trace the pattern onto the fabric first with a pencil.) While the paint is still wet, quickly sprinkle salt over the surface or in particular areas. Always add the salt last to prevent stray crystals from wandering onto other painted areas. Allow the fabric to dry completely, then gently brush the salt off. Do *not* disturb the fabric while it is drying. To stop the salt reaction, turn the fabric—stretcher and all—and tap the back to remove the salt. Then heat-set the paint according to the manufacturer's directions.

You can use different kinds of salt to create distinct effects. Table salt results in a fine, feathery look, while coarse salt produces a more striking effect. (The dramatic starburst pattern on the silk lining for

PAINTING TECHNIQUES TO TRY

It's loads of fun to experiment with different ways of applying paint, as well as mixing-and-matching techniques. Here are some ideas to get you started:

♦ Let paint trickle down wet fabric.

♦ Paint, stamp, or stencil a design on painted fabric.

♦ Scrunch fabric while the paint is still wet to create a textured effect.

♦ Apply liquid acrylic paint from a squeeze bottle with an applicator tip for writing or outlining.

♦ Paint stripes in the watercolor style, then sprinkle salt along the edges.

♦ Add salt to the center of a painted circle to create a flower effect.

♦ Gradate colors from light to dark or dark to light using the watercolor technique.

♦ Paint a different color on each end of the fabric, and gradate the colors to meet in the middle.

♦ Paint pieces of fabric and cut them up. Then reassemble them to create hand-painted patchwork, or use them as appliqués.

the *Southwest Vest* was created using a mixture of fine and coarse salt.) Since pearl salt grains are a uniform size, they create an even, rounded design.

Try experimenting with the amount of salt you use as well. If you use too much salt, the reaction will be hampered. However, if you use too little, the effect will be barely visible.

Using Light-Sensitive Paint

You can use photo- or light-sensitive paint (called heliographic paint) to produce results that are both stunning and unusual. First, the paint is applied to the fabric. Then, while the paint is still wet, stencils or other shapes are placed on top of it. Finally, the fabric is allowed to dry in the sun. Exposure to the sun darkens the colors, but when the stencils or other objects are removed, the areas underneath them are lighter than the background color, creating a contrast and a pattern. (The lapels and binding of the *Southwest Vest* were painted using this technique. The random geometric design was created by placing cardboard templates on the fabric.)

To use this technique, wash the fabric and iron it while it is still damp to remove all the wrinkles. Then place it outside on a flat work surface and moisten it with a sponge. Quickly apply diluted paint with a large brush or sponge. You can paint it in any style, including watercolor, using one or many colors. While the fabric is still wet, lay stencils, shapes cut from cardboard, or other objects on top of it. You can use leaves, feathers, lace, buttons, hardware, or any-

thing else that will mask the fabric and block the light. You can overlap shapes or arrange them in a design. Leave the shapes in place until the fabric is dry, then remove them and heat-set the paint according to the manufacturer's directions. If you want to create shadowy images, move the stencil every 15 minutes as the fabric dries.

MARBLING

The creations of this ancient craft are so enchanting, they seem almost magical. Marbling is created by floating colors (paint) on the surface of a gelatin-like medium (called size), just like oil floating on water. The mottled or streaked patterns that look like marble are produced by manipulating—swirling, raking, or combing—the floating colors, then placing a piece of treated fabric on the colors. The result is essentially a contact print of the marbled pattern. Because each piece of marbled fabric is made individually, a different design is created every time, even when the same colors and techniques are used.

Natural fabrics, such as silks and cottons, are ideal for marbling. Synthetic fabrics can be marbled, though some will be pale. Keep in mind that the tighter the weave of the fabric, the sharper the marbled pattern or image. Fabrics with a nap, like corduroy or velvet, do not marble very successfully.

To practice marbling, start with small pieces of fabric. You can cut them up for piecing, or use them to make two-sided, or reversible, appliqué for other projects. (See "Dimensional Appliqué" in Chapter 2

Amish Diamond Table Runner. *Hand-made marbled fabrics add elegance to this table runner, which features a classic Amish quilt pattern. The technique of marbling fabric is easier than you may think and yields results that are both spectacular and unique.*

for more on this process.) Try pleating or rolling sample pieces and making jewelry from them. Or try marbling fabric that is colored rather than white; just keep in mind that the background color will affect the applied colors. You can even marble objects, including flower pots, tennis shoes, wooden boxes, place mats, and napkins.

Consider inviting a friend to help you marble fabric. It is much easier to work with larger pieces of fabric when two people hold the fabric to lay on the bath. And it's lots more fun if someone is there oohing and aahing with you when you lift each piece of marbled fabric from the bath and view the extraordinary results.

For details on creating different marbling patterns, see the step-by-step directions for the *Amish Diamond Table Runner* beginning on page 81. In this project, the marbled fabrics are cut into large shapes and pieced in a simple design—an effective way to display these beautiful and elaborate patterns to best advantage.

PRINTING

Printing is one of the simplest, most rewarding ways to create a surface design. It's as easy as printing with a potato or a leaf—something nearly all of us learned

Printed Leaf Pillow Materials. *It's possible to create appealing images with the most ordinary materials. This pillow is printed using leaves, wood blocks, and triangles carved from gum erasers.*

to do in grade school. A simple image can be printed in a free-form pattern all over a piece of fabric, or in a geometric pattern.

Object Printing

With object printing, images are made by spreading paint or ink on an object, then pressing the object on the fabric. You can print with almost anything, from fruits and vegetables to hardware or textured items like corrugated cardboard, burlap, and string. You can even print with your fingers or hands. Found objects are especially fun to use for object printing. The next time you are in a fabric shop, study the designs on the fabric and think about found objects that could be used to look like them.

Basic Tips for Printing

For either technique, you need a flat work surface padded with newspaper. (If your work surface is

Printed Leaf Pillow. *Simple techniques can produce exciting results, as shown by this printed and quilted pillow. The design is created using both object and block printing techniques. Note the different textures produced by varying the amount of paint on the printed leaves and triangles.*

not flat, the design will not print evenly on the fabric. Padding increases the "give" of the surface and improves the quality of the image.) Cover the newspaper with a layer of plain paper; brown paper or plain newsprint, available from art supply stores, is ideal. Spread the ink or paint in a Styrofoam tray or on a nonporous surface.

Using a brayer (an inking roller made of hard rubber), roll the paint or ink over the surface of the printing block or object until the surface is covered with a thin coat. (If you are block printing, the paint or ink should cover only the raised part of the design.) For an even print, roll the paint or ink on the surface in one direction, then at a right angle. For a more textured effect, roll it on the surface in different directions. (You can also apply ink or paint—one or more colors—with a brush: Use even strokes or just dab it on.) Then press the painted side of the printing block or object firmly onto the fabric. Some dimensional objects must be rocked back and forth to make contact with the fabric; when you are through printing, lift the object up, taking care not to smudge the image.

An alternative technique is to place the fabric on top of the painted object, then rub over it with the back of a wooden spoon, or apply pressure with a clean brayer. You can print objects like leaves or feathers by applying the painted side to the fabric, with a paper towel on top, and gently rubbing to get an impression. To make a geometric pattern, mark the fabric in a block grid or a diamond grid, then print the image inside the grid lines. (For more on the printing process, see the step-by-step directions for the *Printed Leaf Pillow* beginning on page 85.)

SPRAYING AND SPATTERING

Spraying and spattering are ideal for creating textured surfaces on fabric. These techniques are especially effective when they are used to produce patterns. Both methods are great fun, but—as you may have guessed—they can be very messy! Plan on working outside, if possible. If you have to work indoors, spread paper over both your work area and the floor.

Spraying is quick and easy: Using a plant mister or other sprayer, you simply apply aerosol spray paint or thinned conventional fabric paint to the fabric. There are many kinds of sprayers available. Some spray bottles and misters have an adjustable nozzle, which gives you some control over the paint. For

Sprayed and Spattered Pillow. *The white grid on the background of this pillow is created by using masking tape to keep sprayed and spattered paint off parts of the design. Ivy leaves are also used as a mask. No-sew appliqué leaves complete the design.*

Sprayed and Spattered Pillow Materials. *You can create surprising patterns by flicking paint from a brush or spraying it from a can.*

more sophisticated, controlled results, you can use an airbrush-type applicator.

Most paints need to be diluted before you can spray them. Dilute to one part paint, one part water. Thin more, if necessary. However, remember that colors will run if oversprayed. (Then again, this could be just the look you want.) When spraying the paint, it is generally best to mount the fabric vertically. (The paint generally will not run, because the droplets are so fine.) If you are using spray paint, read the label and take precautions to avoid breathing the fumes. Wear rubber gloves and a painter's mask, and work in a well-ventilated area.

Spattering is a more random and less controllable technique than spraying. Spattered fabric is created by showering the surface with tiny dots and specks of paint from a small brush, such as a toothbrush. This technique can produce varied results, depending on how the paint is applied, how much paint is on the brush, and so forth. Flicking paint from a paintbrush, for example, results in splashes and large flecks of color. Generally, gentle taps of the brush produce fine marks, while bolder movements result in a more pronounced effect. A heavy spatter of a deep color over a lighter color adds depth and vibrance. A fine spatter or spray of black over a lighter color suggests texture.

Basic Tips for Spraying and Spattering

To create a sprayed or spattered pattern, select a paint that is suitable for the fabric you have chosen. Wash the fabric to remove any sizing, then place a mask or template over areas of the fabric you don't want the paint to reach. Spray or spatter paint onto the masked fabric, allow it to dry, and remove the mask.

You can make masks or templates from almost anything. The grid on the *Sprayed and Spattered Pillow*, for example, is created by covering the fabric with masking tape. Try tearing up bits of paper to create clouds, spraying through pieces of lace or screen, or cutting out conventional templates to produce specific images. To prevent the paint from drifting under the fabric, use tape or spray adhesive to secure masks or stencils to the fabric. If you are planning to use a lot of paint to create dark colors, use plastic to make masks or stencils; cardstock or paper will disintegrate or warp if it gets too wet.

You can create wonderful surface designs by overlapping shapes and colors, which gives the illusion of a complicated pattern. For instance, try building up colors by applying layers of sprayed and spattered paint and letting them dry between coats. To blend colors, spray or spatter new layers while the fabric is still wet. Keep in mind that sprayed and spattered colors appear much lighter than painted ones, because the droplets are actually broken-up bits of color; mix the colors dark, or use paint specifically for airbrushing. (Airbrush paints come in more intense colors and flow more easily and smoothly. They also contain binders and are permanent colors.) In addition, remember that thinner fabric tends to absorb color, while thicker fabric produces richer results.

SPONGING

Sponging, another quick way to create textured fabric, produces results that are almost impossible to accomplish with a brush. This technique can be used with muted colors to produce a soft, mottled background or with bright, contrasting colors to create bolder effects. The *Sponged Leaf Pillow* demonstrates how sponging can be used to make a simple textured fabric.

The texture you achieve depends on the type of sponge you are using, its absorbency, and the size of the holes in it. Natural marine sponges create a more

Sponged Leaf Pillow. *Sponging paint or ink on fabric is an excellent way to add texture and interest. This design combines a sponged-fabric frame with no-sew appliqué leaves. A center panel with a quilted grid adds contrasting texture.*

Sponged Leaf Pillow Materials. *Natural sponges add interesting texture because they are so irregular. Synthetic ones can be used to produce uniform, hard-edged prints.*

You can obtain many different effects, depending on the number of colors you use in a design. Use a single color to create a simple texture; for an illusion of depth, use several colors. It's even possible to produce a marbled effect with two-color sponging. Or, try dabbing a sponge in paints that have been swirled together rather than mixed thoroughly. Try letting one color dry before applying a second color—or another coat of the same color. Or apply a new layer while the previous one is still wet. Sponging on a wet surface produces a soft, impressionistic look. If colors turn out too dark, soften them by sponging a second color on top, or by pressing a clean sponge on top of the wet paint to remove some of the color.

STENCILING AND STAMPING

Stenciling and stamping are both great ways to create patterns on fabric without a large investment of time or money. With a little practice, even beginners can obtain professional-looking results with these easy techniques. Both methods allow you to repeat the same image over and over again to produce a pattern, or you can use them to create a single motif.

There really isn't a right or wrong way to stencil or stamp—It's simply a matter of what effect you want to achieve. With stenciling, for example, you can create different effects by varying the type of fabric, as well as the amount of paint and how it is applied. Paint can be sprayed, sponged, or dabbed on with a brush; all produce different results. You can also use several colors to create intricate surface designs. Keep in mind that the smaller or more intricate the design, the tighter the fabric weave should be.

For best results, plan your design before you start to apply the paint or ink. Always read the product information on the paint or ink you plan to use to be sure it will be permanent. Also, test the paint or ink on a sample of your fabric. (You may need to thicken the paint slightly for stenciling and stamping.)

Always start a stenciling or stamping project by washing the fabric to remove any sizing and ironing it while it is still damp to remove any wrinkles. Prepare a flat work surface by padding it with newspaper and a layer of plain paper on top. (Use brown paper or plain newsprint, available from art supply stores.) Secure the fabric to the work surface with masking tape. When you are finished, allow the paint or ink to dry. Heat-set, if necessary, following the manufacturer's directions.

irregular, blended texture than synthetic ones. Each natural sponge has an uneven shape and irregular holes, which produce an interesting textural effect. Synthetic sponges produce uniform, hard-edged prints; you can cut them into shapes, or alternate several sponges to add variety. Compressed sponges are especially easy to cut into shape: Simply draw the desired shape on the sponge, and cut it out with scissors. Then soak the sponge in water to expand it. After it dries, glue it to a stiff board, and you are ready to sponge. If you like this technique, try using crumpled paper, plastic wrap, muslin, or cheesecloth in a similar manner.

The amount of paint on the sponge and the pressure applied also affect the texture. For best results, dab the sponge in the paint, then dab on a piece of scrap fabric a few times to remove any excess paint. Also, try to vary the design. Instead of sponging in distinct rows, sponge an all-over design in a random style, and change the position of the sponge as you print.

STENCILED AND STAMPED BLOCK

This no-sew appliqué block from the *Crazy Quilt Fabric Diary* illustrates several different methods for stenciling and stamping fabric. Purchased children's stencils were used with spray paint to create three oak leaves. (Notice the overlapping motifs, made by moving the stencil and shading the color.) The iris was stenciled with a stencil brush through a brass stencil. Several stamps were incorporated into the design as well. For example, alphabet stamps were used to send the message "I Love You," while simple triangle stamps were used to create an edging. Spiral stamps, gum eraser stamps, and a purchased stamp colored with a fabric marker were also used. All of these techniques are loads of fun, and present endless opportunities for decorating quilts and other projects. Try them all, or experiment with one or two on a crazy-quilt block of your own. Or make a pillow or wall hanging to give as a gift. See Chapter 7 for information on the techniques used on this block, as well as directions for making the *Crazy Quilt Fabric Diary* and a color photo of the completed quilt.

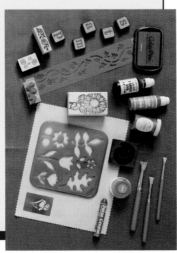

Basic Tips for Stenciling

Stenciling is probably best known as an early-American craft for decorating walls and floors. A stencil—a flat cutout with a pattern of open and closed areas—is placed on a surface, then paint is brushed over the surface. The cut-out portion of the stencil allows paint to pass through, resulting in a painted image on the surface below. Scores of precut stencils—both brass and adhesive-backed types—are available, with anything from flower or fruit motifs to geometric patterns. You can also cut stencils from your own designs.

Stencils can be made using Mylar, clear acetate, oaktag, stiff paper, or self-adhesive paper. (Transparent stencils are convenient, since they allow you to see what you are doing.) You can also use masking tape directly on the fabric as a stencil for straight lines, shapes, and curves, or to isolate an area.

To make a stencil, draw or trace the pattern. (Keep the design simple.) Then tape the stencil material on top of the pattern, and trace around the area to be cut out with a marker. Working on a flat cutting surface, cut the stencil out with a craft knife; turn the stencil material as you are cutting.

For best results, make separate stencils and use separate brushes for each color. To cut a second stencil, follow the same procedure as you did for the first, but make register marks to indicate where to place the pattern when stenciling, so you can align each stencil exactly the same way. Marking the four corners on the pattern, and then again on each stencil, works well. You can also mask or tape (use masking tape or drafting tape) the parts of the stencil that you do *not* want included or that you want to make another color.

Fabric paints, stencil crayons, and stencil creme can all be applied with stencil brushes—stubby, rounded, stiff-bristled brushes specially designed for stenciling. Or you can sponge or spray the paint on.

To stencil fabric, tape down the fabric and use masking tape, drafting tape, or spray adhesive to position and adhere the stencil to it. (If the piece of fabric is too large to tape down, hold the stencil in place near the openings in the stencil, to prevent it from shifting as you apply the paint.) Place a small amount of paint in a shallow container. Dip the entire tip of the applicator, brush, or sponge into the paint. Dab it several times on a piece of fabric or on paper towels until it seems almost dry. Every time you load more color, repeat this process, using a different brush for each color. (Be careful not to use too much paint, or it will get under the stencil and smudge the design.) Begin to stencil the image by applying the paint lightly, using circular strokes, and moving from the edge of the stencil toward the middle. Always hold the brush perpendicular to the surface. When you are finished, gently lift the stencil, taking care not to smudge the paint. To shade a design, begin applying paint in the area you want the darkest, then gradually use less paint on the brush to lighten the color. When cleaning up, be sure to clean both the front and the back of the stencil.

Basic Tips for Stamping

These days, almost everyone knows how fun it is to use rubber stamps. You see stamps just about everywhere—on stationery, personalized greeting cards, even homemade wrapping paper. And you can find stamps with just about anything you can imagine on them, from phrases and sayings to flowers, animals, and famous people. You can print in multicolors, color stamped designs with textile markers, or use a stamp wheel for continuous stamping. Beware of this technique—It can become addictive!

Rubber stamps are the most common and readily available type of stamp, but you can make your own quite easily. Stamps are especially easy to make from erasers. There are also products available that allow you to make your own foam stamp with a ball point pen, a found object, or textured fabric. Or, you can cut out simple shapes from an adhesive-backed material, then bond them to a wood block for stamping. If you are making your own stamps, be sure to cut deep enough to ensure a sharp image.

When stamping fabric, you can apply the paint or ink to the stamp using an absorbent pad or a bottle dabber. (You can also dab the paint or ink onto the stamp with a foam brush. However, this method doesn't work well with detailed stamps, since it blurs the imprint.) As you stamp, use firm, even pressure; do not rock the stamp back and forth. Hold the stamp firmly in place for a second or two, then lift it carefully. Re-ink the stamp and repeat. Allow the ink or paint to dry. Heat-set, if necessary, following the manufacturer's directions.

Clean the stamps each time you change a color, to avoid transferring the wrong color. To clean stamps properly, use a 50/50 solution of window cleaner and water. Wipe the surface of the stamp with an old towel or soft cloth. If you plan to reuse a stamp within a few minutes, you can set it face down on a wet paper towel so the ink doesn't dry out.

Keep in mind that stamp pads do *not* generally contain ink that is permanent on fabric. Make your own by filling a clean foam pad with textile paint, or by layering pieces of felt and filling them with textile paint. There are also many brands of ink available that are specially made for stamping on fabric.

IMAGE TRANSFER

In Victorian times, actual photographs were stitched onto a cotton or linen background and surrounded with floral embroidery. Today, we can transfer photos, letters, paintings, or even comic strips onto a piece of fabric by using a technique called image transfer.

Image transfer generally refers to photo transfer, which involves transferring a photographic image to cloth using an acrylic medium. Sun printing, which uses sunlight to copy an image, is another useful technique. (See "Sun Printing," on p. 77.) Other options for transferring images include transfer papers and pens. With these, you simply trace an image onto special transfer paper and iron it onto the fabric. (One advantage of this technique is that you can throw away any mistakes without wasting fabric.) You can also buy paper for transferring line drawings or designs from paper to fabric. These materials enable you to use a single color copy and make multiple images from it, each lighter than the previous one; printing two lighter transfers on top of one another creates especially interesting color effects. Keep in mind that transfer papers and pens only work on 100-percent polyester or blends with 60 percent or more polyester.

Image transfer is an especially effective way to personalize your work. For example, you can use it to preserve family memories, by including photographs on a quilt block, or to celebrate a special birthday, by using images of birthday candles.

Photo Transfer

With this process, images can be transferred face up or face down. The face-down technique reverses the image, but has the advantage of providing a matte finish, as well as a thinner and more pliable transfer that is machine-washable. The face-up technique does not reverse the image, but produces a glossy finish. (You can spray it with a matte finish, if you like.) The final image cannot be machine-dried, and has a thicker feel, because two layers of medium are needed to achieve the transfer. The greatest advantage of

IMAGE TRANSFER BLOCK

This block from the *Crazy Quilt Fabric Diary* features several different transferred images, all created from photocopies so the originals would not be destroyed. The design includes both black-and-white photographs and a color postcard transferred with a gel medium. A transfer pen was used to trace the line drawing from a book of Bible stories my father had as a child. The feather was created using sun printing. See Chapter 7 for information on the techniques used on this block, as well as directions for making the *Crazy Quilt Fabric Diary* and a color photo of the completed quilt.

this method is that words and numbers are not reversed.

Do *not* use original photographs for this process. Instead, use color photocopies or color photographs from magazines and other publications that have a matte—rather than a glossy—finish. Be sure to make extra copies to experiment with. (Canon laser copiers seem to make the best color copies for transfers.) If you are copying several photographs, fit as many as possible on one sheet and cut them apart later. Keep in mind that you can also enlarge or reduce photographs.

To transfer a photo using the face-up method, lay the photocopy right side up on waxed paper. Brushing in one direction, apply a coat of transfer medium, and allow it to dry until it is clear. Then apply a second coat of medium, brushing in the opposite direction. Allow it to dry overnight. Soak the transfer in water until the paper softens and rubs away from the plastic coating. Lift the transfer carefully and place it on a flat surface. Rub the paper away gently, taking care not to stretch or distort the plastic. After removing the paper, blot the plastic dry with paper towels. Lay the transfer face down on waxed paper. Allow it to dry again. Then trim the transfer, if you wish. To apply the transfer to fabric, brush a thin coat of medium on the wrong side of the transfer. Make sure all of the edges are covered, then immediately adhere the transfer to the fabric. Place paper towels over the transfer, and roll with a rolling pin in all directions to seal the transfer to the fabric. Allow it to dry.

To use the face-down method, trim the photocopy to the exact size desired, then lay it right side up on the waxed paper. Brush on a coat of transfer medium; make sure all of the edges are covered. Spread the medium evenly and thickly (about 1/16″) so you can't see the image through it. On a hard surface, lay the wet transfer on the fabric, and press it down lightly with your fingers. Place paper towels over the transfer, then roll with a rolling pin in all directions to seal the transfer to the fabric. Remove the paper towels. Allow it to dry thoroughly. Soak the image with a wet sponge, or submerge it in water until the paper is wet. Gently rub the center of the image with your fingers until the paper begins to roll. Carefully remove the top layer of paper. Use a sponge to rub off the rest of the paper. Allow the transfer to dry, then coat it with a thin layer of medium to seal it.

Regardless of the method you choose, handle the transfer carefully. If it sticks to itself (which it has a tendency to do), hold it under running water while gently separating it. Keep in mind that it is extremely difficult to sew through the transfer, so apply it to the fabric with the gel and sew around rather than through it. Never iron the transfer or place it in the dryer. To clean, hand wash.

Sun Printing

This is an extremely simple copying technique that creates images almost like magic. It uses specially treated fabric, which produces strong, clear images when it is exposed to sunlight and then rinsed in water. To use sun printing, first find a place to work that is out of the sunlight. Secure the treated fabric (available at some craft stores and by mail-order) to a smooth, flat surface, such as cardboard or foamcore board. Arrange the design elements (flat shapes or dimensional objects) on the treated fabric, then pin them in place, or lay a piece of glass on top to secure them. Set the fabric with the design in the bright sunlight for 5 to 15 minutes to print it. (Do not move either the design or the fabric during this time.) Rinse the fabric thoroughly in water until it runs clear. Dry it indoors, out of direct sunlight. The design will gradually appear as you rinse; it will look brighter when the fabric is dry.

You can develop very interesting effects with this technique. For instance, flat objects will print a crisp-edged outline, while dimensional objects will produce a halftone shadow. If the objects move in the breeze a bit, shadows will form. Think about patterns you can create using found objects and items you have on hand. Netting and laces are obvious choices, but don't limit yourself to these. For example, try using hardware, or masking tape to make a grid. Paper stencils, feathers, grass, and flowers are also effective. The *Image Transfer Block* features a feather printed with this technique.

You can also transfer photographs with sun printing by making a halftone film negative first. To try this technique, use the instructions that come with sun printing materials.

Hand wash sun-printed fabrics with Woolite or Orvis soap; do not wash with a detergent containing phosphates. Drip-dry.

USING PENS AND MARKERS

Fabric pens, textile markers, and permanent pens all provide easy, no-mess ways to draw, outline, and write on fabric. They are also useful for shading images or for adding design details with fine lines that are normally sewn or embroidered. Try using fabric pens and markers to reproduce a piece of line art or clip art, or to add poems, verses, or your own signature to a project. Or, use them to color in stamped or printed images. The *Crazy Quilt Fabric Diary* in Chapter 7 illustrates several ways you can use fabric pens and markers effectively. The completed quilt top was decorated with a border "embroidered" with a fine-tip marker, and quotations were added as well.

Pens and markers come in a variety of thicknesses. Fine-point markers are ideal for drawing architec-

tural lines or for illustrating. (To shade an image by stippling, simply tap the point on the fabric to create dots.) Brush-tip markers are very versatile—Use them to produce broad or fine lines, or to enhance printed and stamped designs by filling them in with color. They're easier to use than a brush and paint, and best of all, there's no mess to clean up! (Many pens and markers come with two points: a fine point on one end and a brush-type nib or an extra-fine tip on the other.) Chisel-tip markers provide precise control and allow you to color a large area quickly. Altering the angle of the tip creates variation in the thickness of the line. Try metallic markers for writing a poem, outlining a shape, or signing your work. There are even empty markers for you to fill yourself to make your own.

When using pens and markers, always start with washed, pressed fabric. Stretch the fabric, then fasten it to your work surface with masking tape. Or, press the shiny side of freezer paper onto the back of the fabric to secure it. (If you don't secure the fabric, it could pull out of shape, or the pen or marker could catch or drag on it.) Draw the design on paper first. Then, using a light box or a window, trace the design with a pencil onto the fabric. Finally, using the pencil lines as a guide, draw or write the design on the fabric with the pen or marker. As you draw, keep a flowing movement, and try not to stiffen up. When filling in larger areas with color, lay the fabric on felt or cotton batting for blending the strokes.

If you plan to use pens or markers, choose a smooth fabric. Cottons work best; polyester blends tend to bleed. With the exception of some permanent metallic pens, markers and pens generally do not work on dark fabrics. Before starting a project, always test the marker you intend to use on a scrap of your fabric. To prevent the fabric from bleeding, try spraying the back of the fabric with a fine mist of sizing or spray starch. You can also help prevent bleeding by using a blow dryer to dry the fabric quickly.

Southwest Vest

This easy-to-make vest demonstrates the versatility of several fabric painting techniques. The soft background colors are created using the watercolor technique; the patterning on the trim and binding, with light-sensitive paint; and the starburst pattern on the lining, with salt crystals. Each method produces a distinct result, yet requires little time or effort. If you like, you can use some or all of these painting techniques, then use other embellishment techniques featured elsewhere in this book to decorate the vest.

The body of the vest is sewn from silk noil, or raw silk. This textured, medium-weight fabric takes paint especially well, resulting in vibrant colors and beautiful surface variations. Silk noil is both hand- and machine-washable (on the gentle cycle, with mild soap). This fabric shrinks, so wash it first. The lining is made from silk habotai (10mm), or China silk, which is a light, translucent, plain-weave fabric especially suited to hand painting.

For this project, I used the Lone Star Style #117 vest pattern from Color Me Patterns by Shirley Fowlkes. However, feel free to use any pattern you like. Follow the pattern requirements for your size when purchasing fabric for the vest, binding, and lining, as well as quilt batting for the vest.

FABRIC AND SUPPLIES

Natural silk noil for vest and bias binding

White habotai silk for lining

Quilt batting for vest

Fabric paint in orange, coral, gold, and strawberry for vest and lining (I used Setasilk)

Transparent light-sensitive paint in red ochre for lapel and bias binding (I used Setacolor)

Salt crystals

Thread

Brushes or sponges

Buttons or other embellishments

Thin cardboard (for making geometric masks for patterning)

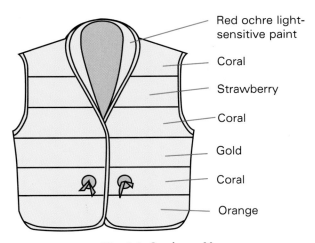

Red ochre light-sensitive paint
Coral
Strawberry
Coral
Gold
Coral
Orange

Fig. 5-1. Southwest Vest

Finished Size. Made from a purchased pattern in any size you desire.

Techniques. Fabric painting using the watercolor, salt crystal, and light-sensitive paint techniques.

MAKING THE VEST

Before making the vest, review the general information on painting techniques earlier in this chapter.

1 Wash and press the fabric. Cut the vest pieces, including the lapel and binding, according to the pattern instructions. Sew the side seams together before painting them, to ensure consistent stripes of color along the entire vest. Cut the bias binding.

2 Mix the paints for the vest fabric. Thin the paint with water to the desired color and consistency.

3 Spread the vest on a padded work surface with the right side of the vest facing up. Then moisten the fabric and paint the body quickly and evenly using a broad brush. (See Figure 5-1 for the color layout.) If the paint appears to be settling in areas on the vest, move to a dry padded surface. When you are finished, let the fabric dry, then heat-set the paint according to the manufacturer's directions.

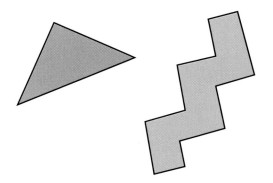

Fig. 5-2. *Vest templates*

4 Wash the lining fabric, then stretch it or tape it down to a flat work surface. Paint it and apply the salt crystals according to the directions under "Salt Crystal Effects" earlier in this chapter.

5 When the lining fabric is dry, cut out the lining pieces according to the pattern. Sew the side seams together.

6 Lay the lining on top of the batting; pin them together, then cut out the batting in one piece.

7 Trace 24 of each of the motifs in Figure 5-2. Then cut them out of lightweight cardboard or any other opaque material.

8 Choose an outside location that receives direct sun. Moisten the lapel and binding with water, then paint them with the light-sensitive paint, following the manufacturer's directions. Place the motifs directly on the lapel and binding, let them dry in the sun, and remove the motifs. Heat-set the paint according to the manufacturer's directions.

9 Sew the vest and lining together, and add the lapels following the pattern instructions. Baste the vest to the batting and lining.

10 Mark the vest for quilting. (See Figure 5-3 for the pattern I used.) Machine-quilt in a free-form pattern with an accent color thread.

11 Add the binding, following the pattern instructions. Add embellishments, if you like.

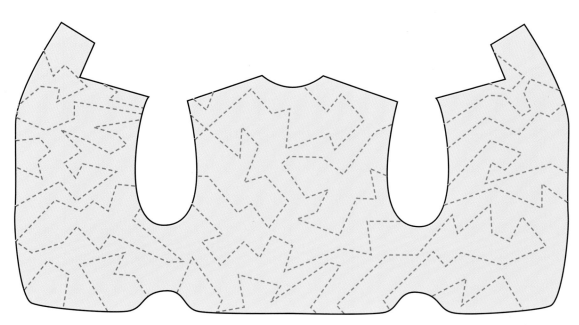

Fig. 5-3. *Vest quilting pattern*

Amish Diamond Table Runner

This elegant table runner provides an ideal way to learn about making marbled fabric. To make this piece, you will create your own fabrics in any colors and patterns you wish. Then you will pick your favorite pieces, choose complementary fabrics to go with them, and sew the pieces together. You can use the runner to overlay a tablecloth, or alone to accent the natural beauty of your table.

This pattern is one of the oldest Amish quilt patterns and is found almost exclusively in Lancaster County, Pennsylvania. Sometimes referred to as Diamond in the Square or Center Diamond, the pattern consists of a large square, tipped on its side, to form the center diamond; large triangles (squares cut across the center on the diagonal) fill in the corners to create another square, which is then outlined by a border.

FABRIC AND SUPPLIES

⅓ yd. marbled fabric 1

½ yd. marbled fabric 2

⅓ yd. marbled fabric 3

⅔ yd. textured fabric 4

¼ yd. solid fabric 5

19″ × 47″ piece of batting

⅔ yd. backing fabric

3½ yds. binding

Alum

Carrageenan

Fabric paint in assorted colors

Tray or cardboard box for marbling

Tools for creating the design (for example, eye droppers, brushes, combs, sticks, or straws)

Newspaper

Finished Size. 17″ × 45″.
Technique. Marbling.

MARBLING THE FABRIC

Although the actual process of marbling fabric is extremely fast and easy, the preparation requires some planning. Start your preparations the night before you intend to marble.

You will need a tray at least several inches larger than the piece of fabric to be marbled. You can use a large plastic storage container with a lid or a photographic developing tray. Or use a roasting pan or line a cardboard box or custom frame with heavy plastic. (If the tray you choose does not have a lid, you can cover it with newspaper or cardboard to keep dust and dirt out overnight.) You will also need a variety of tools to create patterns in the paint, such as combs, skewers, toothpicks, or feathers. To make a comb specifically for patterning, cut a strip of foam-core board to fit the inside width of the tray. Then push T-pins through at evenly spaced intervals.

1 Mix the size (the gelatinous solution used to float the fabric paints on) 12 to 24 hours before marbling. This allows it to thicken properly and lets air bubbles rise to the surface. Carrageenan, a powdered seaweed that becomes a thick liquid when mixed with water, is the easiest size to work with. (It may be hard to find in local craft stores, but can be mail-ordered; see the source list at the end of the book for suppliers.) Mix it following the manufacturer's directions. Normally, you will mix approximately 2 teaspoons of carrageenan with 1 quart of water. Add the carrageenan to the water slowly, making sure it dissolves. (Carrageenan can be mixed in your blender, since it is used to thicken and stabilize foods like ice cream.) Pour the mixture into the tray you intend to use, and cover it to keep it free from dust. There should be at least 2″ of size in the container. You can use size over again if you store it properly; see the manufacturer's recommendations. A typical roasting pan filled with 2″ of size uses less than a gallon of the bath. It can be refrigerated (label it clearly), then allowed to warm to room temperature before using.

2 Prewash the fabric, then pretreat it with an alum solution so the paint will adhere properly. To make the solution, dissolve approximately 2 tablespoons of alum in 1 pint of hot water; cool it to room temperature. Then either dip the prewashed fabric into the alum solution, or sponge the solution on the fabric. Wring the fabric out gently and allow it to drip-dry. Press the fabric before marbling, since

MARBLING PATTERNS

Use the drawings and suggestions below, along with the photo on the facing page, to begin experimenting with marbling patterns.

Fig. 5-4.

Stones. To make this pattern, place drops of paint of various sizes next to one another on the surface of the size bath. You can drop the paint with a squeeze bottle or an eye dropper, or flick it on with a whisk. Do not mix the colors. This pattern is the first basic step for all marbling patterns.

Feather. To make this pattern, start with the stones pattern. Then take a comb or hair pick and draw it through the paint, parallel to the sides of the tray; the results are called a combed pattern. Then draw lines in alternate directions from edge to edge, using a stick, straw, or stylus.

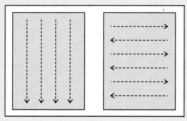

Fig. 5-5.

Zebra. To make this pattern, start with the stones pattern. Take a comb or hair pick and draw it

through the paint, parallel to the sides, to make a combed pattern. Then draw lines in alternate directions from edge to edge, using a stick, straw, or stylus, to make a feather pattern. Finally, repeat the stones pattern by dropping paint on top of the feather pattern.

Free-form. You can combine swirls, zig-zags, and wavy lines with any pattern. Experiment with blending patterns—The possibilities are unlimited!

You can also shadow marble or overmarble fabric that has already been marbled once, to superimpose one design on top of another. Let the marbled fabric dry, re-alum it, then

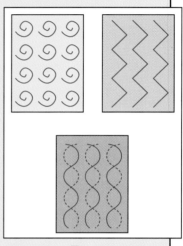

Fig. 5-7.

print again. This is a good way to recycle fabric that does not print well. You can also use this technique instead of cleaning the size bath after each print— Simply print a second time, or else add more color to the remains.

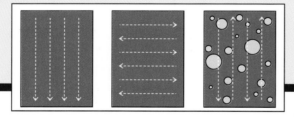

Fig. 5-6.

any wrinkles will affect the pattern. (Do *not* keep alumed fabric for more than a few days, or it will rot. If the fabric pulls apart easily after marbling, too much alum was used.)

3 Before you begin marbling, tear a supply of newspaper strips about 3″ wide and as long as the width of the container. You will need these to skim the surface of the size after marbling each fabric and before adding new paint.

4 Place the paints you intend to use in containers and thin them with water to the consistency of whole milk. When the paint is the right consistency,

it should spread about 2″ to 3″ when placed on the surface of the size. (You want to be able to float the paint on the size so it will create patterns on the surface.) Test the consistency of the paint by laying or lightly dropping it on the surface of the size with an eye dropper, squeeze bottle, or whisk brush. If it is too thick, some (if not all) of the paint will sink to the bottom; thin the paint with water if too much sinks. If it is too thin, it will spread out too quickly and become almost invisible. Most acrylic paints will float and spread without much difficulty, but some colors and some paints do *not* mix. If you have a problem, try using the same brand of paint for all of the colors.

Hand-Marbled Fabrics. *You can achieve a variety of effects with marbling. This photo shows some of the basic marbling patterns, which can be created in an infinite number of color combinations.*

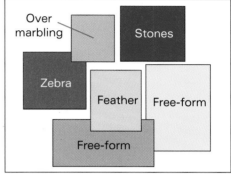

Fig. 5-8. Marbled fabric guide

5 When you have finished testing your paints, skim the size bath with a strip of newspaper. Then drop the first color of paint on the size and let it spread out. Continue adding colors, either next to or on top of the previous colors. As you add more colors, they will intensify because they are being pushed together.

6 When the combination of colors appeals to you, make a pattern by mixing and manipulating the paint on the surface with the tools you collected. (See "Marbling Patterns" for ideas to try.) Consider how the fabric will be used, and try to make the pattern to scale.

7 Step back to evaluate the pattern you have created. Your fabric will look exactly like the pattern on the surface. If you don't like the way the pattern looks on the bath, simply skim the surface to remove the color, and start over. If you like it, remove any air bubbles by touching them gently with your fingertip or pulling them out with an eye dropper. (Be careful not to disturb the pattern!) Bubbles will result in blank spaces on the fabric.

8 Hold opposite ends of the prepared fabric and lay it on the surface of the bath for 2 to 5 seconds. Place the middle down first, and allow the sides to gently roll down. (This prevents air bubbles from appearing underneath the fabric.) Try to do this step in a smooth, even flow, or marks will appear on the fabric. You will be able to see the color soaking through as the fabric absorbs the paint. Do *not* move the fabric after you have placed it on the paint, or the design will be smudged.

9 To remove the fabric, lift it by two corners of the same edge, and drag it along the rim of the container to remove any excess size. Handle the fabric carefully to keep it from folding onto itself.

10 Rinse the fabric thoroughly in cold water to remove the size. Do not wring it out. Lay it flat, or hang it up to dry with clothespins.

11 Once the fabric is dry, let it sit for several days. Then press it on the back to heat-set, following the manufacturer's directions for the paint. Marbled fabric can be gently hand-washed in warm or cold water with mild soap.

12 Skim the surface of the bath with strips of newspaper until it is clean. (Usually once or twice is sufficient to remove the remaining paint.) Then begin the next design. You can use the size again; just store it in the refrigerator in a clearly labeled container. It will start to mold after a couple of days.

MAKING THE TABLE RUNNER

1 Select three pieces of marbled fabric and two complementary fabrics. (I used a light, textural print fabric and a dark solid one.) Then cut out the pieces using the Cutting Chart below as a guide. All pieces include a ¼″ seam allowance.

2 To make the pieced Amish diamond blocks, follow the diagram in Figure 5-9. Sew B triangles on the sides of an A square. Then sew D strips on two sides of this block.

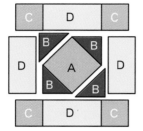

Fig. 5-9. Amish Diamond block

3 Next, make a strip by sewing C squares to either end of two D strips. Sew these strips to the top and bottom of the main block.

4 Repeat the process to make the block for the other end of the runner.

5 Sew E strips on opposite sides of the center square, as shown in Figure 5-10. Then join the Amish diamond blocks to the center square by sewing them to the E strips.

6 To add the border, sew G strips to the top and bottom of the runner. Sew two sets of two H strips together to make two 47″ strips. Sew a 47″ strip on each long side of the runner.

7 To finish the runner, sew the two backing pieces together to create a 47″ × 19″ length. Lay the backing fabric on a flat surface, wrong side up. Place the batting on the backing fabric and then the pieced table runner on top. Baste together, then machine-quilt.

8 Trim the edges to 17″ × 45″. Bind the edges. (See "Binding" in Chapter 7 for binding instructions.)

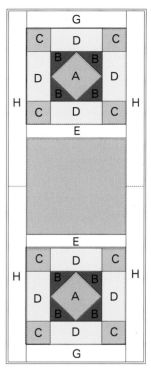

Fig. 5-10. Amish Diamond Table Runner

CUTTING CHART

FABRIC	PIECE	MEASUREMENTS	QUANTITY
Marbled fabric 1	D	8″ x 3″	8
Marbled fabric 2	Center square	13″ square	1
Marbled fabric 3*	A	6″ square	2
	C	3″ square	8
Fabric 4 Light, textured fabric	E	13″ x 2″	2
	G	13″ x 3″	2
	H	24″ x 3″	4
Fabric 5 Dark, solid fabric	B	4½″ squares: Cut 4 squares, then cut them diagonally to form triangles	8 triangles
Batting		47″ x 19″	1
Backing		24″ x 19″	2

*Pieces A and C can be the same or different fabrics.

Printed Leaf Pillow

Pillows are very versatile and have a lot of decorative potential. They are great for projects because they are small and easy to manage, and they don't take a lot of time to complete. Think of them as small canvases for trying out a multitude of creative ideas.

This printed pillow illustrates several different techniques. The central leaf image is an example of object printing. The ivy leaves are printed with blocks, and the two sizes of diamonds are printed from carved gum erasers. The diamonds create a geometric design that complements the leaves: The larger diamonds create a border around the central image, while the smaller diamonds form an all-over pattern.

FABRIC AND SUPPLIES

½ yd. natural muslin

16″ × 16″ piece batting

16″ pillow form

Brayer or brush for inking

Styrofoam tray

Gum erasers

Printing blocks

Paint and ink

Optional: Leaf for central image

Fig. 5-11. Printed Leaf Pillow

Finished Size. 15″ × 15″.
Technique. Printing.

PRINTING THE DESIGN

1 Wash the muslin and press it to remove any wrinkles. Then cut four pieces: You will need two 16″ × 16″ pieces for the front and back of the quilted top of the pillow, and two 12″ × 15½″ pieces for the flaps, which form the back of the pillow.

2 Lightly mark an 8″ square in the middle of the pillow front fabric with pencil. Mark the center point of each side of the square.

3 Put printing ink or paint in a Styrofoam tray or on a nonabsorbent washable surface. Move the roller or brayer back and forth to distribute the paint evenly on the roller.

4 You can print with an actual leaf, or make a leaf design block using the template in Figure 5-12 (page 86). To print with a leaf, choose one that isn't torn, and that fits into the 8″ central square. (Fresh leaves are more pliable and the veins more pronounced, but you can also print with a pressed leaf.) Roll a thin, even coat of paint on the surface of the leaf.

5 Place the leaf, paint side down, on the fabric. Put a clean paper towel on top of the leaf, and rub over the leaf with a clean brayer or the back of a wooden spoon.

6 Remove the paper towel and carefully peel the leaf off the fabric.

7 Using the templates in Figure 5-13 (page 86), cut one 1″ and one ½″ diamond printing block from gum erasers. Cut each ivy leaf from a wood

block or any of the printing blocks you can obtain in craft stores.

8 To print the large diamond border, begin at the center point of one of the sides of the 8″ square you drew around the central image. Print diamonds along the central square toward the corners, using the pencil line as a guide.

9 Print the ivy leaves and ½″ diamonds randomly outside the diamond border. Vary the placement of these images for visual interest.

10 Allow the paint to dry. Heat-set according to the manufacturer's directions.

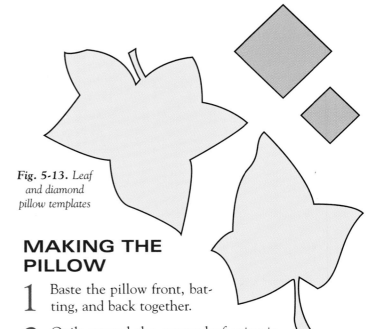

Fig. 5-13. *Leaf and diamond pillow templates*

MAKING THE PILLOW

1 Baste the pillow front, batting, and back together.

2 Quilt around the center leaf print in an echo pattern and ⅛″ around each ivy leaf and large diamond.

3 Trim the quilted pillow front to 15½″ × 15½″.

4 On each 12″ × 15½″ flap, turn one edge under ¼″ and press. Then turn ¼″ under again, press, and topstitch.

5 Place the quilted pillow top face up, and lay Flap 1, wrong side up, over the upper end of the quilted pillow top, as shown in Figure 5-14. Pin in place. Repeat with the right side of Flap 2 on the lower end.

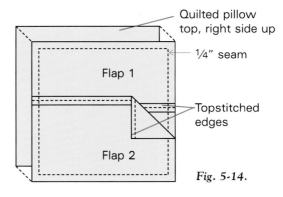

Fig. 5-14.

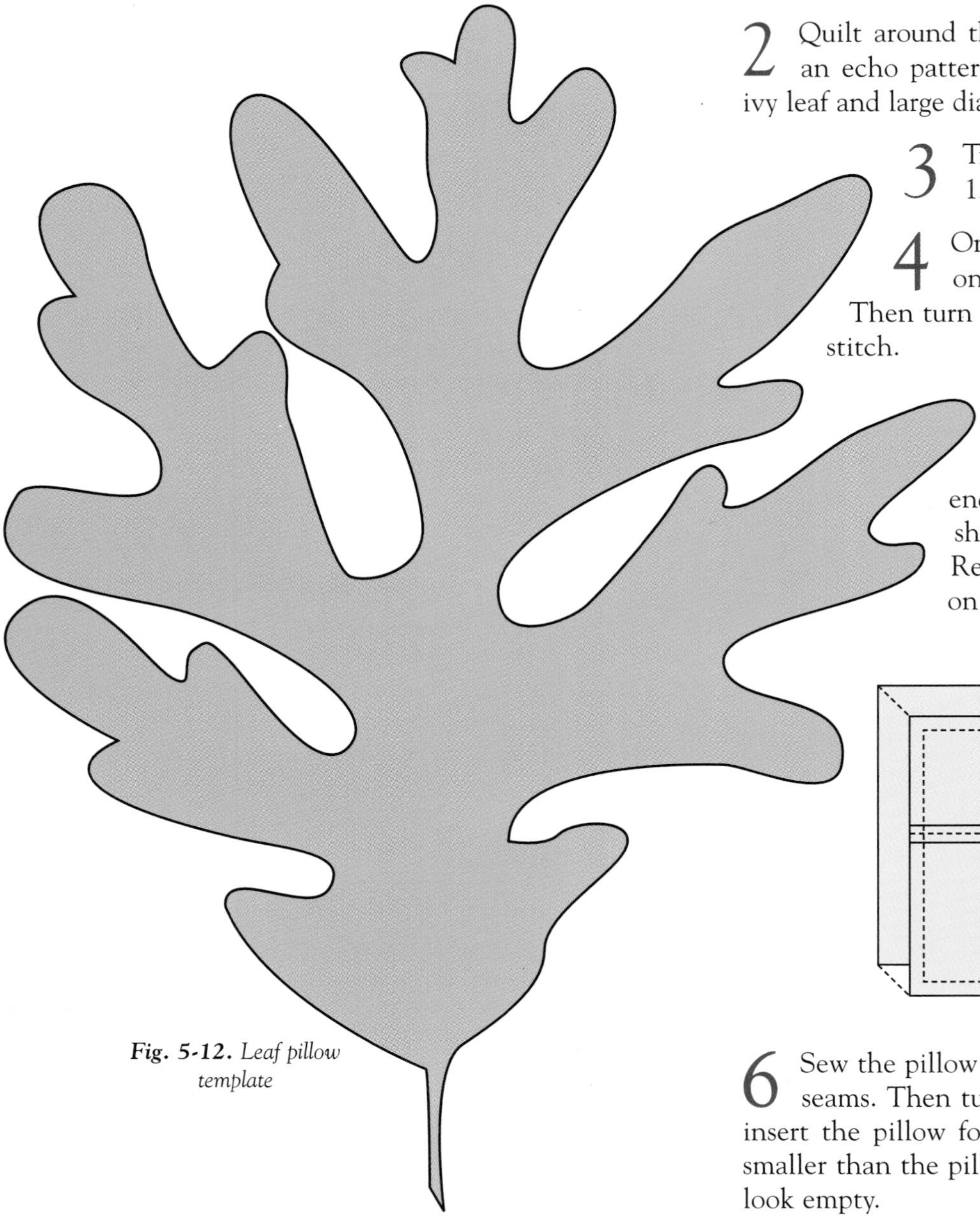

Fig. 5-12. *Leaf pillow template*

6 Sew the pillow top and flaps together with ¼″ seams. Then turn the pillow right side out and insert the pillow form. The cover is made slightly smaller than the pillow form so the corners will not look empty.

Sprayed and Spattered Pillow

This charming pillow features a sprayed and spattered background that contrasts with a white lattice grid. The grid is created by using lines of masking tape to block the paint droplets. A semicircle of earth tone-colored leaves, made using basic no-sew appliqué, completes the design.

FABRIC AND SUPPLIES

½ yd. natural muslin

Scraps of fabric for appliqués

16″ × 16″ piece batting

16″ pillow form

½″-wide masking tape

Fabric paint or ink

Ruler

Soft pencil

Toothbrush, paintbrush, or spray bottle

Stick or piece of heavy cardboard

Optional: Pressed ivy leaves and a vine

Optional: Spray adhesive

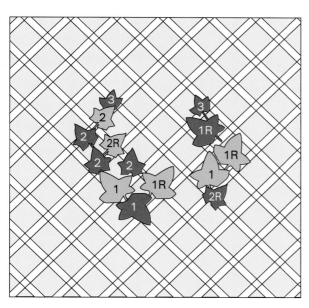

Fig. 5-15. Sprayed and Spattered Pillow

Finished Size. 15″ × 15″.

Techniques. Spraying and spattering paint, as well as basic no-sew appliqué.

CREATING THE DESIGN

1 Wash the muslin and press it to remove any wrinkles. Then cut four pieces: You will need two 16″ × 16″ pieces for the front and back of the quilted top of the pillow, and two 12″ × 15½″ pieces for the flaps, which form the back of the pillow.

2 Using a ruler and a soft pencil, lightly draw a series of diagonal lines 2″ apart across the pillow front fabric. Then draw another series of lines 2″ apart across the fabric in the other direction to create the diamond grid for the lattice (Fig. 5-15). To make the mask for the grid pattern, press a strip of masking tape along each pencil line, first in one direction and then in the other. Be sure to put the tape on the same side of the line each time, so the grid size will be consistent.

3 Lay pressed ivy leaves and a vine in a pattern on top of the masking tape lattice, or cut the leaf shapes out, using the templates in Figure 5-16.

Fig. 5-16. *Leaf templates*

4 Spray or spatter the background pattern, or combine these techniques. To spatter it, use a toothbrush, a stiff brush, or a paintbrush with an all-purpose fabric paint. (Thin paint tends to run more.) Dip the tip of the bristles into the paint, then hold

the brush over the fabric and draw a stick or a piece of cardboard across the bristles. (Be sure to bring the stick toward you; otherwise, you'll be wearing the spatters!) Move the brush to spread the spatters around. (I made the color darkest in the center, and lightest toward the edges.) If you decide to spray the background texture, use spray adhesive to adhere the ivy leaves and vine (Step 3), and mount the fabric vertically. Then spray the paint, holding the sprayer approximately 6″ to 8″ from the fabric.

5 Allow the paint to dry. Remove the tape and leaves. Heat-set the paint according to the manufacturer's directions.

6 Add the appliquéd ivy leaf design on the pillow front, following the pattern in Figure 5-15. Be sure to reverse any leaves marked with an "R" in Figure 5-15.

7 To finish the pillow, follow the steps under "Making the Pillow" for the *Printed Leaf Pillow* on page 86. Quilt through the center of each line in the lattice and around each ivy leaf.

Sponged Leaf Pillow

This pillow features a sponged-fabric border that provides a frame of color and texture around a central panel. The central panel is quilted in a grid pattern to highlight the contrast between the two textures. Leaves, cut from solid as well as sponged fabric, are used to create a central motif. You can enlarge the design in Figure 5-17 and use it as a pattern, or collect leaves to trace for your own design.

FABRIC AND SUPPLIES

½ yd. natural muslin for sponging

½ yd. natural muslin for center square and backing

Scraps of fabric for appliqués: rust (Leaf 1), dark olive (Leaf 2), light olive (Leaf 3)

Piece of natural sponge for sponging for Leaf 4

16″ × 16″ piece batting

16″ pillow form

Natural sponge

Paint and/or ink (rust and raw umber)

Shallow container for paint

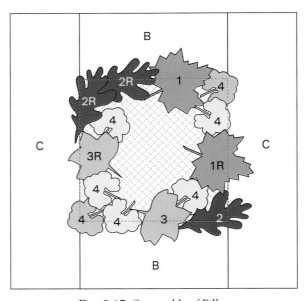

Fig. 5-17. Sponged Leaf Pillow

Finished Size. 15″ × 15″.

Techniques. Sponging, as well as basic no-sew appliqué.

1 Mix the paint in a shallow container. The consistency should be fairly sticky.

2 Wet ½ yard of muslin fabric, then use a natural sponge to apply rust fabric paint on the surface. Dab the sponge in the paint, then on a piece of scrap fabric a few times to test the density of the paint and remove any excess.

3 Wash the sponge thoroughly and squeeze it almost dry. Then sponge the raw umber fabric paint on top of the rust.

CUTTING CHART: LEAF PILLOW C

FABRIC	PIECE	MEASUREMENTS	QUANTITY
Sponged Fabric	C	16" × 4¼"	2
	B	8½" × 4¼"	2
	Flaps*	15½" × 12"	2
Natural muslin	Center square	8½" × 8½"	1
	Backing	16" × 16"	1

*For back of pillow

4 Allow the paint to dry, and heat-set it according to the manufacturer's directions.

5 Following the Cutting Chart above, cut the pieces for the pillow. All pieces include ¼" seam allowances.

6 Sew B strips to the top and bottom of the center square, as shown in Figure 5-17. Press the seams open.

7 Sew C strips to the opposite sides of the center square. Again, press the seams open.

8 Using basic no-sew appliqué techniques, add the leaves to the front of the pillow. To use the design in Figure 5-17 as a pattern, enlarge it until the center panel measures 8½" square.

9 Mark the center square with a ½" diamond grid. (See Step 2 of the *Sprayed and Spattered Pillow* on page 87 for general directions; simply change the grid size.) Baste the pillow front, batting,

and back together. Quilt the grid and around each appliquéd leaf.

10 To finish the pillow, follow the steps under "Making the Pillow" for the *Printed Leaf Pillow* on page 86.

CHAPTER 6

DYEING TECHNIQUES

Dyeing fabric is one of the most versatile techniques available to quilters and crafters. It is a truly magical process, yielding brilliant colors in unlimited combinations. Dyeing a patterned fabric creates entirely new designs. You can even use this technique to enhance a dull bargain fabric that's been languishing in your fabric drawer. Be careful, though—It can become addictive!

Because the dyeing process itself is sometimes quite technical, it can be intimidating. My goal in this chapter is to take the fear out of the process and show you how you can achieve spectacular results with simple techniques. You can use these methods to produce mottled and variegated colors for realistic-looking appliqué leaves, fruits, vegetables, and flowers—even a sky dotted with delicate clouds. Both color washing and overdyeing, for example, enable you to create color patterns that just aren't achievable using other fabric techniques. We'll also explore tea tinting and scrunch dyeing, as well as techniques for removing or discharging color from already-dyed fabric. If you can bake a cake, take comfort: These "recipes" are easier!

ABOUT DYES AND DYEING

Dyes are commonly categorized by their type of bond: Each type of dye will react with specific types of fibers. For example, some dyes work on natural fibers, others on synthetics. The techniques for setting the color vary as well. Unlike fabric paint, which sits on top of the fabric, dye penetrates fabric and becomes part of the fibers, where it is held by either a physical or a chemical bond. As a result, painted fabric has a stiffness, or hand, which dyed fabric does not.

To keep the process simple and the necessary equipment to a minimum, I have used only certain liquid dyes for the projects and techniques in this book. (If you

are interested in learning more about dyeing, there are many books and workshops available.) Which dyes you choose to use will depend on your needs. See the list below or the projects at the end of the chapter for suggestions regarding suitable dyes.

Before you begin dyeing, it will help to know a few key terms. A *dyebath* is the water and dye mixture in which fabric is submerged for dyeing. Dyes that are described as *fast* do not fade in light or water; *fugitive* dyes *do* fade in light or water. A *tint* is a lighter value of a color, created by reducing the amount of dye or adding more water to the dyebath. Any dye can be used as a tint, by diluting it to change the hue or intensity of the color.

Regardless of the type of dye you are using, always wear rubber gloves, an apron, and old clothes. Use a face mask if you are working with powdered dye, and goggles if there is any danger of splashing the dye in your eyes. Always protect your work area—Dye will stain anything it comes in contact with. Keep a damp cloth nearby to wipe up spills. You will need glass, stainless steel, porcelain, or plastic containers for dyeing; label them clearly and use them only for dyeing.

Many brands and types of dyes are available—some for natural fabrics, others for synthetics. Each brand of dye is different, so be sure to follow the manufacturer's directions. I've listed a few of the liquid dyes and discharge agents that I use:

Createx Liquid Cold Water Fiber Reactive Dyes. These can be used on cotton, linen, viscose rayon, and wool for immersion dyeing and direct application. For overdyeing, add the concentrated dye to water containing the fixer. The colors become fixed in the dyebath and need only to be rinsed; no steam setting is required. For color washes, add the concentrated dye to Createx Dye Diluent, which contains all the ingredients necessary for color fixing.

Visionart Instant Set Silk and Wool Dye. This is a concentrate that can be used for immersion dyeing and direct application. It needs to be diluted with a water/catalyst solution. No setting is needed.

Seitec Tumble Dye. This product provides soft, permanent color that can be used on natural or synthetic fabric. No rinsing is required. Heat-set with an iron.

Discharge Paste Color Remover. Use this for removing color on fabric. It has a strong ammonia odor.

Discharge Tumble Dye. This actually removes the color from black or dark-colored garments and replaces it with another color.

Procion Dyes. If you want to use powdered dyes, use these. They are not much more difficult to work with than liquid dyes, but be sure to use a face mask to avoid breathing the powder. Also, beware: The powder is so fine, particles can easily blow on other items in the work area.

TEA TINTING

Tea tinting, or tea dyeing, is a remarkably quick and easy technique that is also surprisingly versatile. It is especially useful for blending colors, by muting or toning them down. For example, if you want to use a floral print in Broderie Perse appliqué but the print has too much contrast in the motif (bright white fabric can be very difficult to use), try tea tinting to tone down the contrast. Or use it to take away the harshness of garish colors—bright yellows and greens in a fish motif, for instance—that clash with your other fabrics.

White and light-colored fabrics are altered the most by this technique, while dark fabrics are barely changed by it—if they are changed at all. Tea tinting creates shades of brown and gives white fabric an ivory appearance, producing a charming antique effect. Try it to antique a beautiful piece of lace, or to simply add a range of muted tones to fabrics. You can tea tint individual pieces of fabric or an entire project after it is completed.

Tea Tinting Basics

When tea tinting, start by washing the fabric to remove any sizing. For best results, use 100-percent cotton fabric; cotton-polyester blends usually dye well but take longer to absorb the color. Always test a swatch of your fabric first, and dry the sample to make sure the tint is correct. If you are planning to tint purchased or finished pieces, like the Battenburg

VICTORIAN TABLE LINENS

Antique Victorian linens, from fancy pillow shams to delicate doilies, are quite fashionable today—probably as much as they were in our grandmothers' day. With tea tinting and Broderie Perse appliqué, you can create your own "antique" linens. These table linens were created from a purchased set of white, 100-percent cotton Battenburg Lace linens. The four place mats, four napkins, one small round linen, and one larger round linen were tinted with 20 tea bags in 1 gallon of water and allowed to soak for 15 minutes.

Each linen has a different floral motif, all cut from the same length of fabric and fused onto the linens using the Broderie Perse technique described in Chapter 2. The motifs are arranged asymmetrically, adding variety and interest to the collection. To make your own set of linens, select a fabric with a motif that is appropriate for your color scheme. (For this set, I used approximately ¼ yard of fabric and ¼ yard of paper-backed fusible web. If you are planning to make a larger set, estimate how much material you will need as closely as possible, and always have extra on hand.) Battenburg Lace, also known as Renaissance Lace, is quite easy to care for: Wash it with mild soap in warm or cold water, roll in a towel, then dry flat. Press while slightly damp, using a press cloth for the lacework.

Lace table linens used for the *Victorian Table Linens*, test a similar fabric to see if the tint gives the desired results.

You can either purchase commercially packaged tea dye, or mix your own. To make tea dye, bring 1 gallon of water to a boil in a large pot. Add tea bags—use more for a darker tint, fewer for a lighter tint—and boil, covered, for about 20 minutes. Remove the tea bags and stir. Place the wet fabric into the tea bath and let it soak, stirring every 5 minutes, until the desired color is reached. (The fabric will dry lighter than it appears when it is wet.) Most fabrics need to soak about 10 to 30 minutes in the bath, depending on the depth of color desired. Wash the fabric in a mild soap after tinting; otherwise, the acid in the tea may deteriorate your fabric over time. Press to set the color.

Several variables can affect the results of tea tinting: the type of tea, the amount of tea used, the amount of water, the amount of fabric, and the length of dyeing time. To create a series of fabrics with a gradation of tints, keep all the variables the same, but change the number of tea bags each time. For example, start with 5 tea bags for the first bath, then add 10 the next time, and so on. The tones will get darker and richer as you add tea bags. Keep records and swatches for reference so you can recreate the results. If you want a really "antiqued" look, add loose tea grains to the tea bath, and leave them in with the fabric; darker stains will form wherever the grains touch the fabric.

COLOR WASHING AND OVERDYEING

How many times have you found the right fabric pattern and design, only to discover that the color was totally wrong? With color washing and overdyeing, you are no longer limited by the choices available in fabric stores. These two techniques allow you to add color to a solid color fabric, or even a printed one, simply by redyeing it. Both are quick and easy methods for creating the exact fabric you need for your project.

Dyes are transparent colors that blend with the existing color of a piece of fabric, allowing you to place one color over another. Color washing and overdyeing specifically use diluted color to soften, enhance, and modify the colors underneath. Like tea tinting, these methods are useful for changing high-contrast fabrics to more subtle or subdued tones. The basic concept is the same for both techniques, but

Nantucket Fabric Painting. *Color washing, overdyeing, and scrunch dyeing are all used to make unique custom fabrics for this wall hanging of a Nantucket lighthouse. These techniques are ideal for creating intense hues, as well as natural-looking textures and colors*

the method of application differs: Color washing is accomplished by brushing or sponging dye directly onto a colored or printed fabric; overdyeing involves immersing the fabric.

The results of either technique depend on the color of dye used as well as the color of the original fabric. (The type of dye used and the fiber content of the fabric also have an effect.) Experiment with various colors of dyes and fabrics, and keep samples of your original fabric as a reference. Remember: You cannot lighten a color once it is applied, so experiment on swatches before tackling a large piece of fabric.

As you experiment, you'll find that light dyes will not have much of an effect on dark colors. However, dark dyes over light colors will produce an obvious effect. For example, if yellow fabric is dyed with a red dye, it will turn orange, but dyeing a red fabric with yellow will not change the color much. A yellow fabric overdyed with blue will turn green, not blue. (Only black will cover other colors.) Overdyeing or applying a color wash to a printed design will not cause the design to disappear; rather, all the colors on the fabric will be altered. Fabrics with a lighter background, including pastels, are the best choices for these techniques.

When trying these methods, you will also discover that not all the dye will fix to the fabric. To remove the excess dye, first rinse the fabric in cold water until the water runs clear. Then rinse in hot water until the water runs clear again. Wash with a mild detergent, rinse, and dry. Do not wash the dyed fabric with other items until you are sure the excess dye has been removed completely.

Color Washing Basics

Color washing involves brushing or sponging dye directly onto a colored or printed fabric that has been stretched on a frame or other prepared surface. Depending on the size brush you use, this process creates a pattern of large brush strokes or finer lines, similar to a watercolor effect. It is best for smaller pieces of fabric or for times when you want to create brush strokes on the fabric. The thinner and smoother the fabric, the faster the color will flow across it.

To color wash a piece of fabric, wash it in hot water and detergent to remove sizing. Stretch the fabric on a frame, or place it on a prepared surface by layering several thicknesses of newspaper and covering them with plain (unprinted) newsprint or paper towels. Prepare the dye according to the manufacturer's directions, then apply the color with a brush or sponge. Load the brush with color, but don't use *too* much dye, or the color will flood your design. You can brush evenly from side to side or make obvious brush strokes, depending on the look you want to create. By applying the color freely, you can overlay colors and blur the edges; careful brushing will give you more precise lines.

If you want to avoid the appearance of hard edges, you can also wet the fabric before you apply the wash. Wetting the fabric causes the brush strokes to merge into the fabric, and dilutes the color of the dye somewhat, too. However, if the fabric becomes *too* wet, puddles will occur; dab it with a sponge and allow it to dry slightly before continuing.

Dye for color washing can vary in consistency from a paint-type of concentration (dye thickened with a medium) to a mixture that looks like tinted water (dye thinned with diluent). To thicken dye, try adding a dye painting medium; the dye will spread more slowly, resulting in sharper edges along the brush strokes. You can also add diluent or diffusant to thin dye. Thinning dye is useful for creating lighter values and for preparing dye for spraying or airbrushing.

When color washing, you can create gradations of color from light to dark or dark to light. First, prepare several shades of a color. Then, starting with either the lightest or the darkest color, apply the dye

FABRIC DYEING GUIDE

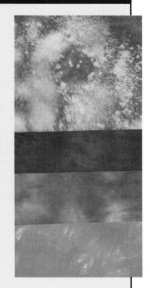

The photo at right shows different fabrics that have been dyed to create a variety of effects. On the top, the large piece was sprayed with a chlorine bleach discharge solution while the fabric was wet, creating a negative pattern of cloudlike shapes on what was originally blue fabric. The bottom three fabrics were all scrunch dyed.

All the samples, in the photo on the left, are paired with the original fabrics so you can see the effect created by overdyeing and color washing. The two pairs of samples on top are the fabrics from the *Galaxy Wall Quilt* in Chapter 4. The dark fabric was overdyed with a deep blue-violet color; the medium fabric was overdyed with a medium sky blue color.

The three samples on the bottom are all from the *Nantucket Fabric Painting*. A tone-on-tone white fabric was overdyed with gray to create a wood-grain color and texture for the frame. In the center, a turquoise color wash was used on the watercolor-looking tree line fabric, to deepen the color and tone down the brighter values. Finally, a light green wash was brushed over the gray print sea grass fabric to give it more depth and intensity

as described above, making a smooth transition from one shade to the next. To vary the shades even more, go back over an area once it is dry and apply more color.

Overdyeing Basics

With overdyeing, a solid color or printed fabric is immersed in a dyebath to create a new solid color or pattern. (Conventional dyeing usually begins with a white or natural-colored fabric.) Generally, a diluted dye is used. Overdyeing is best for a large piece of fabric, since immersing it in a dyebath is easier than brushing the dye onto it.

To overdye a piece of fabric, wash it in hot water and detergent to remove sizing. Prepare the dyebath, following the manufacturer's directions. Wet the fabric, then add it to the dyebath. (Wet fabric absorbs the color more evenly.) Leave the fabric in the dyebath for the specified amount of time: With some dyes, the fabric is removed temporarily from the dyebath so the fixer can be added; with others, you can simply move the fabric to the side of the dyebath and add the required amount of dissolved fixative. (Do not put the fixative directly onto the fabric.) Remove the fabric when it is slightly darker than the desired color. Rinse thoroughly, until the water runs clear. Some dyes require heat setting.

SCRUNCH DYEING

Scrunch dyeing produces a mottled, variegated effect that resembles natural forms, such as clouds or water. This technique is also useful for creating a textured background with subtle effects (say, for a landscape), or for simply adding interest to a solid fabric. You can even use this method to make bold colors and patterns for cutting up and rearranging in a quilt.

Scrunch dyeing involves scrunching or crushing the fabric, stuffing it into a jar, then pouring dye over the compressed fabric. It is a resist type of dyeing, which means that the dye is prevented from reaching certain areas of the fabric, resulting in a unique pattern of dyed and undyed areas. The tighter the fabric is scrunched, the harder it will be for the dye to reach those areas. Folding, tying, and crumpling fabric before it's scrunched into the jar also limits the flow of dye to certain parts of the fabric. You can create many fantastic effects by folding, twisting, and scrunching fabric in different ways. (Tie-dyeing also falls into the category of resist dyeing. Although this technique is commonly associated with T-shirts and '60s artifacts, it's possible to create exquisite designs by using intricate combinations of ties, folds, and twists.)

The sky and water fabrics featured on the *Nantucket Fabric Painting* are dyed using this tech-nique. The fabric for the *Galaxy Wall Quilt* is also created using this process.

Scrunch Dyeing Basics

To scrunch dye, start by washing the fabric in hot water and detergent to remove any sizing. Prepare the dyebath according to the manufacturer's directions. Wear rubber gloves, an apron, and a face mask; be sure to wear goggles if there is any danger of dye splashing in your eyes. Cover your work area with newspapers or a drop cloth.

Next, scrunch the fabric. Keep in mind that the way the fabric is scrunched will determine the finished look. Try scrunching with a specific design in mind, incorporating tie-dye techniques, as well as twisting, tying, or folding. The tighter the scrunch, the more mottled the fabric will be. Dry fabric will tend to produce a more variegated effect, while wet fabric will absorb the dye faster and more evenly. White fabric will dye the truest; gray fabric will have a more toned-down look; dark fabric will retain the dark color and have only a shading from the dye. Be prepared for the unexpected—Surprises make this technique interesting and exciting!

Scrunch or stuff the fabric tightly into a glass jar. Be sure to use a jar that is small enough to compress the fabric otherwise, the fabric will open up too much and you won't get a mottled effect. Pour the dye mixture into the jar until the fabric is covered. (Remember to add the fixer to the dye according to the manufacturer's directions.) Let it sit—there is no need to stir—until the fabric is slightly darker than the desired color.

Rinse the fabric thoroughly to remove any excess color. Rinse in cold water first, until the water runs clear. Then rinse in hot water, again until the water runs clear. Wash with a mild detergent; rinse and dry. Do not wash the dyed fabric with other items until you are sure the excess dye has been removed completely.

DISCHARGE DYEING

Discharge dyeing, sometimes called controlled bleaching, is a technique that uses chlorine bleach or another discharge agent to remove color from fabric. It can be used to create a negative design (a light pattern on a dark surface), or to prepare a piece of fabric for redyeing. Once the fabric is discharge dyed, you can use paint, dye, or markers on the discharged areas or on the entire surface to create marvelous color effects.

Cornucopia Block. *Discharge dyeing was used to create the unique colors and patterns in this block from the* Way-Beyond Baltimore Album Quilt.

Cornucopia Block *fabrics. These samples show just a few of the unlimited patterns you can create by painting, spraying, or spattering chlorine bleach onto fabric. (The original fabrics are on the left of each pair.) One advantage of this process is that the color of the discharge-dyed fabric is always compatible with the original fabric.*

You can apply the bleach solution (discharge agent) to the fabric any way you like, including spraying, drawing, painting, or sponging. Try spattering or spraying bleach over blue fabric for a night-sky effect. Apply the discharge agent with sponge cutouts for texture. Or use discharge paste to print or stamp designs onto fabric. You can also use scrunching techniques or simply immerse the fabric in the bleach solution. After applying the bleach, soak the fabric in a vinegar bath to neutralize the bleach and prevent the fabric from deteriorating.

The color you end up with will depend entirely on the base color of the fabric. For example, two navy fabrics from different manufacturers can result in totally distinct colors, depending on the base dye color. On one, discharged areas might come out a coffee color, while on the other they could turn a soft teal color. When choosing fabrics for this technique, remember that the negative color always works well with the ground color, since it comes from the same color base. There is even a specially treated fabric that is sold commercially and recommended for discharge dyeing, called pima broadcloth. This fabric is available in navy and black, and the discharge results range from shades of gray to brown to cream.

Discharge dyeing is not a precise technique, so try to be open to the results. Sometimes the accidents are pleasant surprises! However, you should always test a sample first. You may need to test several fabrics to obtain the results you are looking for.

Discharge Dyeing Basics

Always start with fabric that has been washed and dried. Fill buckets or other containers with water, and keep them handy for rinsing. You'll also need a vinegar solution for neutralizing the bleach (mix equal parts of white vinegar and water).

To discharge dye, you can use chlorine bleach, discharge paste color removers, or discharge dyes. I recommend chlorine bleach—It's the safest, least expensive, and most readily available discharge agent. (Use only chlorine bleach; non-chlorine bleaching agents do not affect dyes.) Start with a solution of half chlorine bleach and half water, then experiment with other bleach/water solutions; you can use bleach full-strength or dilute it, depending on the contrast you want. To create gradations of color, try different solutions on one piece of fabric. Always test a piece of fabric before you discharge dye the entire piece; otherwise, you won't have any way of knowing which dyes will discharge. (Not all dyes will discharge, though most industrial and fiber-reactive dyes will. Hand-dyed fabrics are almost always easier to discharge.) Do not overbleach (look for signs of the fabric thinning), or it will damage the fabric.

Remember: Discharge products are chemicals.

Use them carefully, always keep them away from children, and follow the manufacturer's directions. When you discharge dye, wear rubber gloves, an apron, and a face mask; use goggles if there is any danger of the dye splashing in your eyes. Cover your work area with newspapers or a drop cloth.

To brush on the chlorine bleach solution, use a broad or thin brush, or a sponge. Dip it in the bleach solution and paint as you would with paint or dye. Be careful not to drop any of the solution on the fabric accidentally—It will discharge the dye and make spots. When you are finished, wash the brushes with soap and water.

If you prefer to spray, fill a recycled spray bottle or plant mister with the solution, and spray the fabric until you have achieved the desired effect. (Always test the sprayer with water first to determine if the spray is fine or spotted, and select the spray setting you want. Be sure to mark the container clearly, and do not use it for anything else.) You can also use the scrunch-dyeing technique, described earlier in this chapter, and simply substitute chlorine bleach solution for dye.

When you apply the solution to the fabric, the bleaching action will begin immediately. The color will be lightest at the point where the bleach is applied. (If you wet the fabric before applying the solution, the bleach will spread more and produce a more subtle, blurred edge.) When the fabric has lightened to the desired value, rinse it in clear water, then place it in the vinegar solution and allow it to soak for 10 minutes. After the vinegar rinse, wash the fabric with a mild soap, and dry.

Nantucket Fabric Painting

This lighthouse wall hanging features custom fabrics created using different dyeing techniques. The sea grass and tree line fabrics, which form the background for all the other pieces, are made using color wash. The weathered wood-style frame is created by overdyeing a white tone-on-tone fabric with medium gray dye. The water and sky fabrics are both scrunch dyed. Although you can also make this hanging from purchased fabrics, it's more fun to dye your own. In fact, dyeing fabric is an exciting, immensely satisfying process. See "Fabric Dyeing Guide" on page 93 for a guide to the fabrics and the methods used to dye them. If you would like to try creating your own fabric painting from a treasured photograph, painting, or drawing, see "Designing a Fabric Painting" in Chapter 1.

FABRIC AND SUPPLIES

⅓ yd. blue fabric for sky

⅓ yd. blue fabric for water

⅛ yd. green fabric for tree line

⅓ yd. print fabric for Broderie Perse sea grass

Scraps of several different light, medium, and dark fabrics for rocks

¼ yd. white fabric for lighthouse, railing, and seagulls

Scraps of dark blue, red, gray, and putty fabrics for the water and lighthouse

1 yd. white-on-white print fabric for frame

⅔ yd. backing fabric

19″ × 26″ piece of batting

½ yd. paper-backed fusible web

⅔ yd. of ⅜″ paper-backed fusible web tape

4 canvas stretchers: 2 measuring 19″ and 2 measuring 26″

Textile marker or fabric pen

Fabric dyes

Brushes or sponges

Finished size. 14″ × 21″ central image; 19″ × 26″, including the border (stretched over the frame). Before stretching, it is 24″ × 31″.

Techniques. This project features fabrics that have been color washed, overdyed, and scrunch dyed. It also uses basic no-sew appliqué and Broderie Perse (described in Chapter 2), as well as supplies such as fabric pens, textile markers, and permanent pens.

Pattern. Page 126.

MAKING THE FABRIC PAINTING

1 Prewash all the fabrics to be dyed for the project. Then color wash the fabrics for the sea grass and tree line. Overdye the fabric for the frame, and scrunch dye the fabric for the sky and water.

Fig. 6-1. Nantucket Fabric Painting

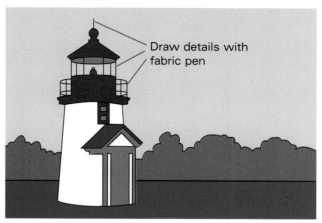

Fig. 6-3.

2 To create the background, fuse the water fabric to the sky fabric using ⅜″ paper-backed fusible web tape. Using basic no-sew appliqué, trace the tree line on paper-backed fusible web. Fuse it to the back of the tree line fabric. Cut it out, then fuse it in place along the horizon line, as shown in Figure 6-2.

Fig. 6-4.

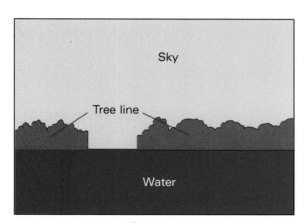

Fig. 6-2.

5 To make the railing, fuse paper-backed fusible web to the back of the white fabric and cut ⅛″ strips of fabric. Fuse them in place, as shown in Figure 6-5.

3 Appliqué the lighthouse, using basic no-sew appliqué (Fig. 6-3). Fuse the main structure in place, then add the top, roofs, window, and doors. Add the detail lines (the black railings and the antenna) with a textile marker or fabric pen. Or you can embroider or satin-stitch them on.

4 Make the seagulls and rocks using no-sew appliqué (Fig. 6-4). Fuse the seagulls to the background. Place the rocks on the background in the area where they are to go. (You will fuse them when you have adjusted the layout to work with the sea grass in Step 6.)

Fig. 6-5.

Cut out grass so railing, water, and rocks show through

Fig. 6-6.

6 The sea grass is made using Broderie Perse. (See "Broderie Perse" in Chapter 2 for a review of this technique.) Cut the sea grass out, then move the rocks around to fit behind the grass. Cut out areas of grass to let the rocks, railing, and water show between the blades of grass (Fig. 6-6). You don't need to cut along the edges of the fabric pattern perfectly; the print will provide an illusion and carry the effect. Be daring: The grass doesn't have to be fused all in one piece. You can always add another layer of grass if you have cut too much away.

7 To make the mitered border, first cut two 5″ × 24″ strips and two 5″ × 31″ strips. Working on the back side of the fabric, find the center of each strip and measure from the center toward the ends. Mark a 45-degree angle; add a ¼″ seam allowance to prevent any gaps when the other border strips are added. Then cut the angled edges off (Fig. 6-7).

8 Apply ⅜″ paper-backed fusible web tape to the back side of the fabric, along the 14½″ edge and on each angled edge. Remove the paper and fuse onto the fabric painting (Fig. 6-8). Repeat the procedure for the border strips on the top and bottom, only this time cut the angle to the exact size, omitting the ¼″ allowance.

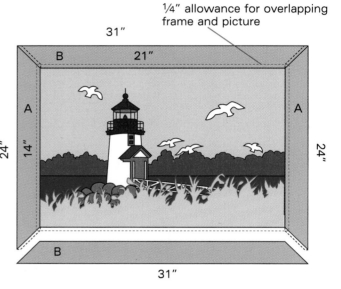

¼″ allowance for overlapping frame and picture

Fig. 6-8.

9 Mark the top of the fabric painting for quilting. Lay the backing, right side down, on a flat surface. Layer with the batting and the fabric painting. Baste and quilt following the design on the pattern.

10 Stretch the quilted piece over canvas stretchers until it measures approximately 19″ x 26″, including the border. The border around the actual fabric painting should be about 2½″.

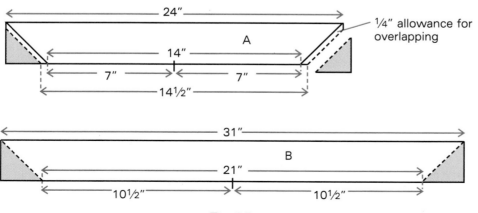

Fig. 6-7.

Cornucopia Block

Discharge-dyed fabrics are the main feature of this block. Different techniques for applying the chlorine bleach are used to create a variety of effects. For example, the fine lines on the cornucopia and the grape leaf are drawn with a brush dipped in chlorine bleach. The fabric for the pumpkin is created using a sponge. Begin the projects by discharge dyeing the fabrics. You can either work directly on the fabric freehand or lightly mark areas to be discharged with chalk. The directions describe the treatments for each fabric, but you can also experiment with scraps to create your own colors. (Of course, you can make this block with purchased fabric, if you like.) The color photo on page 95 will help you decide what effects to try for.

FABRIC AND SUPPLIES

13″ × 16″ dark plum fabric for background fabric

½ yd. paper-backed fusible web

1 yd. gold twisted cord for the tendrils

Fabric glue

Liquid fray preventative

Chlorine bleach

White vinegar

Buckets or containers

Medium-tip paintbrush

Sponge

Spray bottle

Scraps of fabric for central image *or* follow fabric suggestions below

¼ yd. yellow ochre for cornucopia horn

¼ yd. coffee for inside cornucopia and stems

¼ yd. butterscotch for cornucopia rim

¼ yd. green for leaves for leaf 1, 2, 4, 5, 6

⅛ yd. mint green for leaf 3

⅛ yd. red for apples (7 & 8)

⅛ yd. plum for plums (9 & 10)

⅛ yd. peach for peaches (11, 12, & 13)

⅛ yd. dark purple for grapes

⅛ yd. light purple for grapes

⅛ yd. orange for pumpkin

⅛ yd. yellow for pears

Finished Size. Block: 12″ × 15″. This is Block F from the *Way-Beyond Baltimore Album Quilt*, which is 38″ × 44″.

Techniques. Discharge dyeing and basic no-sew appliqué, as well as spraying and spattering.

Pattern. Page 127.

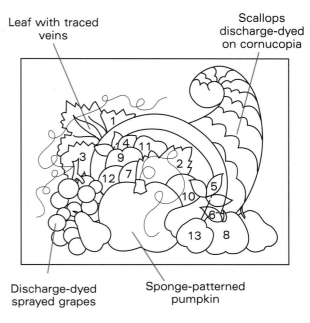

Leaf with traced veins

Scallops discharge-dyed on cornucopia

Discharge-dyed sprayed grapes

Sponge-patterned pumpkin

Fig. 6-9. Cornucopia Block

MAKING THE BLOCK

1 Wash and dry all the fabrics to prepare them for discharge dyeing. Prepare a solution of chlorine bleach, and a vinegar/water (50-50) solution for neutralizing the discharge solution. Have buckets of clear water on hand for rinsing each piece of fabric. After discharging each piece, rinse it in water, then soak it in the vinegar and water solution for 10 minutes. Wash the fabric in mild soap and water.

2 To discharge dye a pattern on the yellow ochre fabric for the cornucopia horn, first trace the cornucopia and the scallop pattern onto the fabric with chalk. Then "draw" the scallops with a medium-tip paintbrush that has been dipped into the dis-

charge solution. Extend the lines slightly beyond the actual shape of the cornucopia. Spray the entire piece of fabric with the discharge solution to create a textured surface (Fig. 6-10).

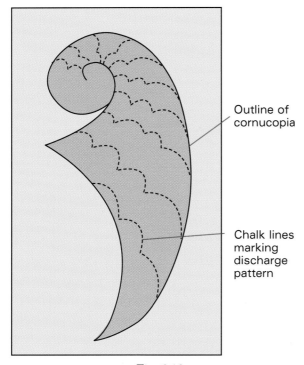

Outline of cornucopia

Chalk lines marking discharge pattern

Fig. 6-10.

3 Wet the coffee-colored fabric for the stems and the inside of the cornucopia, and spray it with the discharge solution.

4 For leaf 1 trace the veins onto the fabric with chalk, or freehand the pattern. Draw the veins with a medium-tip brush that has been dipped into the discharge solution. For variation, brush a solid area with the solution in leaves 4 and 5. Then spray the entire fabric with the discharge solution.

5 Spray the entire piece of mint green fabric for leaf 3 with the discharge solution.

6 Wet the red fabric for the apples (7 and 8), then spray it with the discharge solution.

7 Wet the plum fabric for the plums (9 and 10), then spray it with the discharge solution. Neutralize it immediately for only a slight variation in the color

8 Scrunch dye the peach fabric for the peaches (11, 12, and 13) very briefly in the discharge solution.

9 For the dark purple for the grapes, spray some areas lightly, some more heavily, with the discharge solution. Use a fine mist for some parts of the fabric and large spatters on other parts.

10 Paint the orange fabric for the pumpkin with the discharge solution using a small sponge. Be sure to wipe the sponge along the edge of the container to avoid flooding the fabric. You can draw the shape of the pumpkin on the fabric and then trace the pumpkin's contours to create a more rounded shape.

11 After the fabrics are discharge dyed, use basic no-sew appliqué techniques to trace and cut out all the pieces from the selected fabrics. (Remember to reverse the designs.) Fuse the shapes to the background fabric, working from the background to the foreground. Fuse leaves 1 and 3 in place first, then the cornucopia, and finally the fruits and stems. Glue the cording for the tendrils in place last. Note that the numbers do not correspond to the placement, but rather to the motifs for color and discharge dyeing.

CHAPTER 7

FINISHING YOUR WORK

The way a quilt or other project is finished can have a major impact on its success. That's why the best designers consider how to finish their work while they are designing it. In this chapter, you will find general information on quilting, tying, binding, displaying, and cleaning your work. (For a more in-depth treatment of these subjects, see "Recommended Reading" at the end of this book, or consult your local library.)

In addition, you will find complete directions for assembling the *Way-Beyond Baltimore Album Quilt*. The blocks for this wall hanging, featured throughout this book, demonstrate many ways to use the no-sew techniques I've discussed. I've also included instructions for making the *Crazy Quilt Fabric Diary*. Making your own crazy quilt is an ideal way to practice and perfect all the new techniques you have learned in this book. I hope both projects will inspire you to begin experimenting and to create your own no-sew special effects.

QUILTING YOUR DESIGNS

Quilting is easy to take for granted, but it is much more than simply the stitches that hold the top, batting, and backing of a quilt together. Quilting forms a pattern of decorative stitches that adds surface texture to the cloth. Whether you quilt a project by hand or by machine (or have someone else do the quilting for you), think about how the stitches themselves can serve as an embellishment and function as an important element in the overall design.

Take a minute to look at the quilting patterns used in some of the projects in this book to see the different effects that can be created. For example, The *Way-Beyond Baltimore Album Quilt* features a very simple quilting pattern because the design itself is so elaborate. The quilting stitches in the *Vase with Lilies Wall Hanging* add embellishment and a sec-

Way-Beyond Baltimore Album Quilt. *The blocks in this wall hanging are made using many of the no-sew special effects presented in this book. The colorful prairie points along the central image add a finished look and help unify the design by repeating the colors in the individual blocks.*

ondary design to the project. In the *Sponged Leaf Pillow*, the diamond grid quilting pattern in the center block provides a contrast to the leaf design. The *Printed Leaf Pillow* uses echo quilting, which outlines the shape (in this case, the center leaf) in a repeating pattern and adds dimension by "puffing up" the outlined shape. The quilting in the *Nantucket Fabric Painting* defines the details of the clouds in the sky.

Whether you use a repetitive design like a grid, a free-form pattern, or stitches to outline and emphasize shapes, quilting brings life and adds movement and emotion to a design. Quilting stitches can also produce a subtle relief pattern on the quilt's surface; many stitches in one area will flatten that area, causing other areas where the stitches are less dense to "puff up." In addition, stitches can be used to define details in an image. For example, you can use lines of stitches to create movement in an area of sky or water. They can also be used to delineate architectural features like roof tiles, or to highlight details in nature, such as veins in a leaf. Altering the surface with quilting stitches creates a play of light and shadow, resulting in a dimensional effect.

Machine versus Hand Quilting

Whether you quilt by machine or by hand will depend on several factors. For example, in addition to the design and finished look you want for your piece, you'll need to consider what you intend to use it for. If it's an heirloom piece, you may want to take the time to hand quilt it. On the other hand, if you are making a baby quilt, a table runner, or a piece of clothing that will be used heavily or washed regularly, it's probably better to machine quilt it. The type of fabric you are working with is also important. Machine quilting is more suitable for thick or textured fabrics or polished cottons, since these are hard to hand quilt; thinner, finer fabrics, such as muslin, are easier to hand quilt. Also, if you are working with printed fabrics, you may want to choose machine quilting, since quilting does not show up as well on printed fabrics as on solid color fabrics.

If you plan to quilt with novelty threads, you will probably have better luck machine quilting than quilting by hand: Just be sure to follow the thread manufacturer's guidelines for needle size and tension requirements. Machine quilting is especially suitable for fast and easy stitches, such as straight line and free-motion quilting; decorative stitches are also interesting to use on the machine.

Of course, your decision to machine or hand quilt will depend on the time you have available, too. Machine quilting is generally faster, but it requires some patience before starting a piece. Many people who have the time find hand quilting very relaxing.

Basic Quilting Steps

Regardless of whether you are quilting by hand or using the machine, there are a few basic steps you must understand in order to quilt successfully:

1 **Mark the fabric.** Before you begin to quilt, you'll need to mark the fabric. Materials for marking fabric range from chalk and slivers of soap to water-soluble pens and mechanical or lead pencils. Chalk markers tend to rub off easily, although some of the colors can be difficult to remove. If you use soap, you can harden it in the refrigerator first. (Do *not* use soap with cream in it.) To remove soap, just use a damp cloth or wash the piece. Water-soluble pens can work well, but always test them on the fabric first. Or try mechanical or lead pencils for light fabrics and silver pencils for dark fabrics; they are generally easy to wash out, or you can erase them with a fabric eraser.

You can also use cardboard and adhesive templates for marking fabric. Freezer paper templates can be ironed down. Con-Tac paper can be pressed in place. Stencils and patterns are handy for marking patterns, too.

Choose whatever marking method suits you. Just be sure to test on a scrap of fabric first. Also, consider marking the top before basting the layers together; it's easier to mark on a hard surface than on top of the batting and backing.

2 **Add the Batting and Backing.** After marking the fabric, you need to add the batting and backing. Choose a flat surface, then lay the backing fabric down, right side down. Lay the batting on top of the backing; add the top, right side up. Working from the center out, baste this "fabric sandwich" together using thread, safety pins, or a tacking tool such as QuilTak. Baste every 4" to 6" to prevent the layers from moving around.

3 **Machine or hand quilt.** To machine quilt, always work on a small sample piece first. The results will vary, depending on the sewing machine, thread, and fabric used. If the piece you are quilting is large, roll or fold it so it will be easier to handle. Start by making a stitch, then bringing the bobbin thread to the top. Hold both threads as you begin, to prevent loose threads and clumps from forming on the back. Keep the needle down when you turn the fabric. Be sure to use the correct size needle for the thread you are using. When sewing curvilinear lines or free-motion quilting, use a darning foot with the feed dog down. When sewing straight lines, use a walking foot.

To hand quilt, place your "fabric sandwich" in a quilt frame or hoop. Then, using the method of quilting stitch that suits you, make small, uniform stitches. (For information on the various methods of making a quilting stitch, see "Recommended Reading" at the end of this book, or visit your local library.)

KNOTTING OR TYING

Another option for securing the layers of a quilt that is fast and not too tedious is tying or knotting them together. This technique, traditionally used for finishing crazy quilts, is especially suitable for thick or heavy fabrics like velvets, corduroys, and even layered fabrics. Thick, puffy batting can also be secured this way.

Common materials used for knotting or tying include thread, yarn, cording, embroidery floss, and ribbons. When choosing a particular material for tying, consider how it will look with the fabrics in the piece. The ties don't have to blend with the fabrics, but they should complement them. (Keep in mind that you can also use ties for special effects— for example, for attaching buttons or charms.) The ties should also have the same care requirements as the fabrics; if the piece is machine-washable, the ties should be, too. In addition, make sure the tying material you are considering is strong enough to keep from breaking when it is tied tightly, yet thin enough to pull through the fabric. It is best to avoid certain ribbons, twisted threads, and other materials that tend to fray, since your knots could easily come apart.

To tie a quilt, layer the top, batting, and backing together, as described in "Basic Quilting Steps" above. Thread an upholstery needle with tying material, then make a ¼" running stitch. Backstitch in the same holes, leaving 2" to 3" tails. Tie the tail and trim it. Once you have mastered this basic technique, try variations (tying the material in a bow, or knotting with long tails, for example) to create different effects.

BATTING AND BACKING

Whether you are quilting or tying the pieces together, the batting and backing should be several inches larger than the quilt top. (Both quilting and tying tend to "shrink" the piece slightly, depending on the amount of quilting and knots.) In addition, batting and backing fabrics should have the same general care requirements as the fabrics, and be compatible with the top.

There are many kinds of batting, ranging from natural fibers like cotton, wool, and silk, to high-loft polyesters and blends. When selecting the batting for your project, consider how you want the finished piece to look, as well as how it will be cleaned. Check the manufacturer's recommendations for uses, cleaning, and so forth. (Many packaged battings can be unrolled and placed in the dryer at low temperatures to fluff them up and take away the creases.) Your choice of batting will also depend on whether you will be quilting or tying the pieces. In general, thick, puffy (high-loft) batting is good for tying and knotting, but not for fine quilting. Batting with a low loft is suitable for hand and machine quilting, as well as for clothing. Cotton flannel is often used in clothing and wall pieces.

The backing can be used as a continuation of the front design, or it can serve as an additional "canvas" to design on. For larger quilts and other projects, piece panels of fabric together to create the backing.

BINDING

The binding not only protects and finishes the edges, it also frames the piece. Therefore, it should enhance your work and add to the overall design. The binding can be contrasting, as in the *Whimsical Cat and Dog Banners*, or it can blend with the border fabric, as in the *Crazy Quilt Fabric Diary*. It can also be the same fabric as the border, as in the *Way-Beyond Baltimore Album Quilt*. Study other quilts and pieces to see what you like and what is effective.

The binding technique used most often in this book is the straight-grain double-fold method: Cut 2" wide strips of fabric lengthwise along the grain. Fold the strips in half lengthwise, wrong sides together. Press. Unfold, then turn each of the raw edges under ½" toward the center, and press. (Instead of pressing by hand, try using a tape-making tool, available at sewing stores. These handy gadgets are very useful for making different widths of binding.)

Bias binding is useful for projects with curved edges and corners, where flexibility is required: Fold a square of fabric into a triangle. Mark parallel lines at equal intervals along the fold, then cut long the lines. (Do not use the fold of the fabric; cut it off.) Fold and press as you would for straight-grain binding.

All the binding for projects in this book is cut in 2" wide strips and folded to ½" wide (the measurement of the finished binding). You can use either individual strips of binding or continuous binding. To make a continuous length of binding, sew the strips together after cutting them out, and before folding and pressing.

There are several methods for attaching binding. Self-binding (as in the *Crazy Quilt*) and overlapped corners (as in the *Whimsical Cat and Dog Banners*) are two of the easiest. To self-bind a quilt, make the backing fabric 1″ longer than the top fabric. Press under the raw edge, then fold the fabric over the front of the quilt and stitch it down. To bind by overlapping corners, lay the binding on the quilt front, right sides together. Stitch along the seam line. Fold the binding over the quilt edge, then fold the raw edge. Stitch the folded edge to the backing fabric.

Banner Binding

Once you have bound a project, it's easy to figure out how to bind anything you make. Here are step-by-step directions for binding for the *Whimsical Cat and Dog Banners* to get you started.

1   Cut two 15½″ × 2″ strips, two 18″ × 2″ strips, and three 7″ × 2″ strips for each banner. Cut the strips lengthwise along the grain of the fabric.

2   Fold the strips in half lengthwise, wrong sides together. Press. Unfold, then turn each of the raw edges under ½″ toward the center, and press.

3   On the 18″ strips, fuse ⅜″ paper-back fusible web tape along the pressed edges on the inside of the binding, as shown in Figure 7-1. On the 7″ strips for the tabs, fuse the ⅜″ paper-back fusible web tape along only one pressed edge. On the 15½″ strips for the top and bottom of the banner, fold the ends under ¼″ and press, then fuse the ⅜″ paper-backed fusible web in place to finish the raw edges.

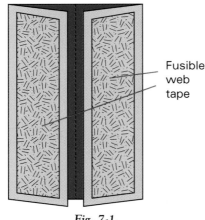

Fusible web tape

Fig. 7-1.

4   Remove the paper backing along one edge only. Fuse onto the front side of the banner along the 18″ edge first. Turn the banner over and repeat on the back of the banner.

5   Add the binding on the top and bottom of the banner.

6   To add the tabs, make a mark at the 5″ and 10″ points on the back of the banner. Remove the paper backing on the three 7″ strips of binding; fuse the binding together. Fold the strips in half and finger press. Starting at the far side of the banner, fuse or glue one back side of one end of a 7″ strip in place. Then fuse or glue the front side of the other end at the 5″ mark. Repeat, starting directly alongside the first tab.

DISPLAYING YOUR WORK

When displaying or hanging quilts or other textiles, use common sense. Avoid displaying them in direct sunlight, which can fade the color of the fabric very quickly. Do not use nails, push pins, tacks, or clothespins, since they could stress or damage the fabric.

Several hanging methods are suitable for the projects in this book. The most common way to display larger quilts or hangings is to use a "sleeve." A sleeve is a tube of fabric, about 2″ smaller than the width of the actual piece, that is hand-sewn to the back of the hanging, under the binding. (It's important to stitch the sleeve on carefully, to avoid sewing through to the front of the piece.) A rod or dowel is inserted into the sleeve, and the piece is hung from the rod. Sometimes referred to as a rod pocket, it helps prevent uneven stress on the fabric from the weight of the hanging itself.

Quilts and other hangings are also commonly displayed using Velcro. Simply glue or staple the hook side of the Velcro onto a strip of wood, then secure the wood to the wall. Hand sew the other side of the Velcro to the back of the quilt or project.

You can also use loops or tabs to hang pieces. They can even be incorporated as an integral part of the design. (The *Whimsical Cat and Dog Banners* in Chapter 2 feature this type of hanger.) Many different materials are suitable for use as tabs or loops, including ribbons, braids, trims, and pieces of binding fabric. You can use curtain rods, brass or copper tubing, or bamboo poles for the rod. If possible, try to blend these materials with the work being exhibited.

To attach a loop or tab, determine its finished length, then double that length and add ½″ (for attaching the loop in the seam). Fold the length in half, matching the raw edges. Sew or adhere either the raw edges or the folded edge under the binding. If the raw edges are attached, a loop will be formed; if the folded edge is attached, the two strips can be tied in a bow or a knot. (Seal the raw edges with fray preventative, or finish them in some other way.) Insert the loop in the seam, then finish the binding.

Stretching fabric over a frame is an attractive way to present your work. Artist's canvas stretchers come in scores of lengths, at 1″ intervals, and can be constructed in any size combination. Quilted pieces, like the *Nantucket Fabric Painting* in Chapter 6, are especially attractive when finished in this fashion. You can also add a sophisticated touch to your work by mounting the fabric on a piece of corrugated cardboard or adhesive foamcore board, then adding a frame without glass. (Precut frames are available at many art and craft supply stores and are easy to put together.)

To stretch fabric over canvas stretchers or a foamcore board, start with stretchers or a mounting board that is the finished size of your project. If you like, you can pad your work by cutting a piece of batting, fleece, or padding approximately 1″ larger than the board or 2″ larger than the stretchers. Lay the padding face down on a flat surface. Center the stretchers or board face down on top. Trim the corners diagonally to avoid bulk. Bring the padding around the edges to the back, then glue or tape it down with masking tape.

Trim the edges of your completed project evenly, allowing 1″ to 3″ on each side, depending on the depth of the stretchers or mounting board. Lay the project, face down, on a clean, flat surface, then center the stretchers or board, face down, on the wrong side of the project. Fold the top edge of the project over, and then the bottom edge, and tape it in place with masking tape on the board, or staples on the stretchers. Turn the project around carefully and make sure it is centered; adjust the positioning, if necessary.

Trim the corners diagonally to reduce the bulk. (Make a mitered corner for the least amount of bulk.) Fold the edges on the sides over, and tape or staple them in place. To finish the back, cut a piece of fabric the same size as the back. Press the edges under approximately ¼″ and glue or sew it in place.

SIGNING YOUR WORK

Be sure to sign your work in some manner. Your signature is important, since it documents the quilt or project by recording the name of the creator. It's nice to add the date, too. Your signature can go on the front or the back, whichever you prefer. You can stamp or stencil a label, sign the quilt by hand with a permanent fabric pen, or embroider your signature. You can also write down other pertinent information, including your comments and thoughts, to pass along with the piece. Simply add these on the back, or record them separately.

CLEANING YOUR WORK

Cleaning textiles can be tricky. For best results, use the method that puts the least amount of stress on the fabric as possible. Also, remember to prewash all fabrics to remove sizing before constructing the piece.

The best way to clean most pieces is to hand wash them with a mild soap and cold or warm water. Rinse several times, gently squeeze the excess water out, and lay flat to dry. To prevent fading, avoid drying anything in direct sun. Many pieces can be machine-washed on the gentle cycle; remove immediately and dry on the fluff or air cycle.

Spray a fabric protectant on wall hangings when you finish and mount them. To clean them, simply brush lightly with a feather duster, or shake them gently.

You can clean embellished pieces with a hand-held vacuum cleaner, by placing a nylon stocking or netting over the nozzle to reduce the suction. Or lay a screen or netting on top of the piece before vacuuming it. If you are embellishing clothing, test all the embellishments and adhesives before making the piece. If you are considering having your project dry cleaned, talk with your dry cleaner about the materials in your piece, and check the labels on the adhesives you used.

Way-Beyond Baltimore Album Quilt

Baltimore Album Quilts have long been used to display a quilter's skill and creativity. Traditionally, they have featured floral themes and incorporated colorful fabrics that are manipulated in many imaginative ways. This project continues in that tradition—with one major difference. Baltimore Album Quilts normally take hundreds of hours to complete. The Way-Beyond Baltimore Album Quilt, on the other hand, uses fast and easy no-sew adaptations of traditional appliqué, fabric manipulation, and embellishment techniques. As a result, you can create a visually exciting piece in much less time!

All of the blocks for this hanging were introduced as individual projects in earlier chapters. If you have already made these, you are ready to finish your quilt: Simply follow the directions below. You can also use this project as an inspiration for your own creations. Why not try some or all of the techniques in this book to create your own Baltimore Album Quilt?

FABRIC AND SUPPLIES

1⅓ yds. dark plum fabric for border and binding

1½ yds. fabric for backing

Scraps of fabric from the various blocks for prairie points

40" × 46" piece of batting

For directions on making the individual blocks, see the following:

Pennsylvania Dutch Flowers Block, page 31

Full-Blown Flowers Block, page 36

Morning Glory Block, page 43

Woven Basket of Flowers Block, page 49

Bird Nest Block, page 61

Cornucopia Block, page 99

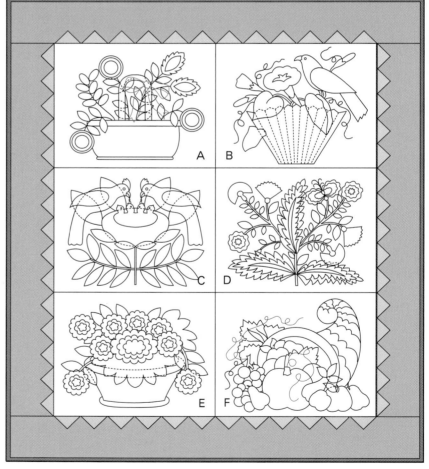

Fig. 7-2. Way-Beyond Baltimore Album Quilt

ASSEMBLING THE QUILT TOP

1 Trim all six blocks for this quilt (listed above) to 12½" × 15½".

2 Using Figure 7-2 as a guide, sew together the following pairs of blocks: A and B, C and D, E and F. Allow ¼" for all seams.

3 Sew the three pairs together to form the quilt top.

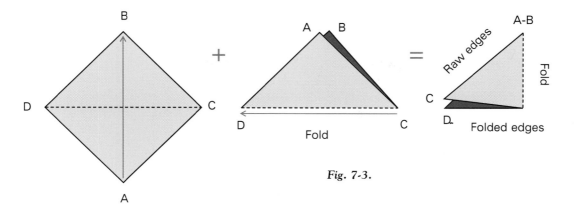

Fig. 7-3.

4 To add color and appeal to the border, make prairie points from different fabrics that were used in the blocks. To make a prairie point, cut a 3″ square of fabric (or any size you want). Fold it in half across the diagonal (point A to point B, as shown in Figure 7-3), and press. Next, fold it in half again diagonally (point C to point D), and press. You should now have a smaller triangle with raw edges all on one side. (The raw edges are sewn into the seam when the border is added to the blocks.) Make at least 54 prairie points.

5 Cut two 5″ × 37″ strips and two 5″ × 40″ strips from the dark plum fabric for the border.

6 Working on a flat surface, lay the border strips in place. Lay the prairie points along the strips to determine the arrangement of colors you would like to use. Arrange the points so the raw edges and the folded edges all face the same direction. Slip the A-B point of one prairie point between the C-D fold-ed edges, overlapping them slightly; the stitching line will be where the two prairie points meet. There should be 12 prairie points across the top and bot-tom, and 15 along each side. You can adjust the placement to fit the length.

7 Pin the prairie points to the border strips. Baste them in place, with all of the raw edges along one side.

8 Sew one 5″ × 37″ strip to each side of the quilt top. Then sew one 5″ × 40″ strip to the top and the bottom. Allow ¼″ for the seams.

9 Mark the top for quilting. (Because the blocks themselves are quite intricate, try to keep the quilting simple. I used two rows of quilting to outline the prairie points. I also made a grid pattern along the seams of the blocks by quilting one row in the ditch between the blocks and another row ½″ on either side of the seam.)

10 Layer the top on the batting and backing, then quilt.

11 Trim the edges to 38″ × 44″, then add a con-tinuous straight-grain double-fold binding: Cut four 48″ × 2″ wide strips lengthwise along the grain from dark plum fabric. (If you like, you can use the same piece of fabric that the border strips were cut from.) Sew the strips together to make a contin-uous length. Fold the strips in half lengthwise, wrong sides together. Press. Unfold, then turn each of the raw edges under ½″ toward the center, and press. Sew the binding to the quilt front, then fold over the edge to the back, and hand sew or fuse to the back of the quilt.

12 Sign the piece and prepare it for display. Spray with a fabric protectant.

Crazy Quilt Fabric Diary

Quilts, by their very nature, are fabric diaries. They can contain swatches of fabric from a treasured friend, a snippet from a wedding gown or other outfit to commemorate a special occasion, and even found objects. Crazy quilts are especially suited to creating your own personal record of events, experiences, and observations. They can reflect current trends of fabric design and color, political and social attitudes, or popular techniques. They are usually decorative rather than functional and feature irregular shapes and sizes of fabrics arranged randomly in a "crazy" pattern. Traditionally, they feature fabrics of different weights, textures, and colors, allowing for a combination of silk, velvet, brocade, and other fancy fabrics not generally used in a traditional quilt.

This crazy quilt is made using basic no-sew appliqué and features many of the embellishing techniques covered in this book. I hope you will use this project as a jumping-off point for experimenting with new techniques. Since crazy quilts have a free-form design and there is no pattern to follow, you can be totally spontaneous with your arrangement. You will find that they provide a wonderful background for embellishing and decorating, and are well adapted to a wide range of no-sew techniques. You can be ornate or simple, dramatic or subtle—Use your imagination!

FABRIC AND SUPPLIES

5 - 7 coordinating fabrics of different textures and values

1⅓ yds. muslin for foundation

1⅓ yds. fabric for border

42″ × 56″ piece batting
(Batting can be anything from a fluffy batting to a flannel sheet)

42″ × 56″ piece of fabric for backing/self-binding

Thread or yarn for knotting

1⅓ yds. paper-backed fusible web

Fabric pens, textile markers, and permanent markers

Embellishments to place over edges (for example, trims, braids, found objects, beads, appliqués)

Liquid fray preventative

Materials for attaching embellishments, including fabric glue and pieces of fusible web tape

Crazy Quilt Fabric Diary. *Ties are used in this wall hanging not only to secure the layers, but also to add embellishments, by attaching charms.*

Finished size. 38″ × 52″; individual blocks are 15″ × 22″.

Techniques. Basic no-sew appliqué; embellishing with laces, linens, and appliqués; embellishing with charms and found objects; stenciling and stamping; image transfer; and using fabric pens, textile markers, and permanent pens.

MAKING THE BLOCKS

I have found the best way to design a crazy quilt block is to play around with the fabrics until you create a pleasing arrangement of shapes and colors.

Instead of trying to recreate my blocks, try making your own design. If you start with soft colors that are fairly close in value (I used beiges, whites, and ivory), the various surface design techniques used to embellish the blocks will have greater visual impact. Generally, solid colors and muted prints work better than bold fabrics. (If you use prints, consider the scale of the print.) Although there will not be much contrast in color in the basic blocks, you can add plenty of color and appeal with the various appliqués and other embellishments.

Once you have selected the fabrics you would like to use for the patches, follow these steps for making the blocks:

1 The blocks are constructed on a piece of foundation fabric that is 2″ larger than the finished block. Cut a 17″ × 24″ piece of foundation fabric for each block. (If you would like to work with a different size block, determine the block size, then add 1″ to each side for the foundation fabric.)

2 Fuse paper-backed fusible web to the back of the fabrics you have selected for the patches. Cut the fabrics into random sizes and shapes to accommodate the appliqués, charms, found objects, stencils, or stamps you plan to use. Remove the paper backing. (For heavier or thicker fabrics, fuse paper-backed fusible web tape along the edges of the fabric only.)

3 Working directly on the foundation fabric, start in one corner and position the first shaped piece in place. Pin it, then add more randomly shaped pieces to the foundation fabric. (Or, if you prefer, start in the center of the foundation fabric and work out to the edges.) Overlap the edges slightly, as shown in Figure 7-4.

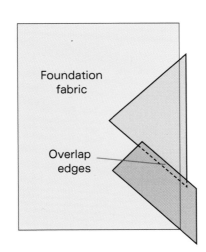

Foundation fabric

Overlap edges

Fig. 7-4.

4 Fuse the pieces in place.

5 Apply liquid fray preventative to raw edges that may ravel. Then embellish the patches any way you please. You can use fabric glue to attach charms and found objects, or tie or sew them in place. Layer on appliqués with fusible web or fusible web tape, or use iron-on appliqués. Arrange buttons or trims along the raw edges. Use these blocks to experiment with any of the techniques presented in this book.

(See "Guide to the *Crazy Quilt Fabric Diary*" for a complete list of the embellishments I used.)

ASSEMBLING THE QUILT

1 Trim all the blocks to 15½″ × 22½″. Using ¼″ seam allowances, sew the blocks together in pairs, then sew the pairs together to create the quilt top. Press the seams apart.

2 Cut two 4¼″ × 44½″ strips for the two side borders, and two 4¼″ × 38½″ strips for the top and bottom borders.

3 Embellish the borders any way you like. You may wish to add embellishments both before and after you sew the borders on. (I added decorative "stitches" with a fabric pen around the individual blocks, along with a variety of charms and sequins, Borderie Perse, and stamped images.)

4 Join the two 44½″ borders to the sides of the quilt top, then the two 38½″ borders to the top and bottom of the quilt top.

5 Working on a flat surface, lay the backing fabric face down. Place the batting on the backing fabric, then place the quilt top over it. Baste with safety pins, or tack in place. Tie or knot the three layers together.

6 Bind the quilt using the self-binding method: Fold the raw edge of the backing ½″, then bring it over on top of the quilt top. Pin in place, then machine or hand sew. (The binding can also be fused in place with paper-backed fusible web tape, as in the *Whimsical Cat and Dog Banners*.)

GUIDE TO THE *CRAZY QUILT FABRIC DIARY*

Use the illustrations and numbered lists that follow to learn more about many of the embellishment techniques used on the blocks for the *Crazy Quilt Fabric Diary*. I knotted a variety of buttons and charms onto the quilt as I tied the layers together. In addition, I used various trims to decorate the seams between patches and between blocks. To further embellish the quilt, I used a permanent fabric pen to draw decorative embroidery "stitches" onto the quilt face—both around the blocks and along the raw edges of several patches. Along the borders, I added

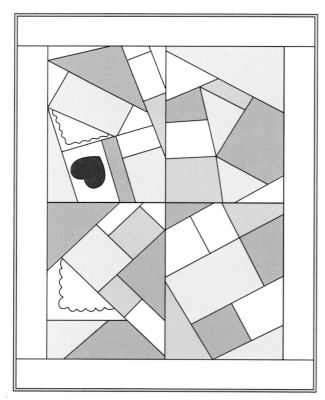

Fig. 7-5. Crazy Quilt Fabric Diary

hand-printed quotations. I used fabric pens and textile markers with different tips to add color to stamped designs on the lower left-hand border. The morning glory in the bottom left corner was created with image transfer, which I then stippled with a fabric marker to add color. (Note: Only worn or damaged antique textiles were used for this project.)

Stenciled and Stamped Block

This block features a variety of images created using stenciling and stamping techniques. (See "Stenciling and Stamping" in Chapter 5 for complete information on these techniques.)

1 The leaf design along the edge was made by placing several colors of paint side by side

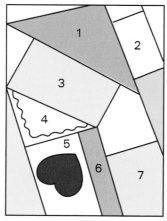

Fig. 7-6. Stenciled and Stamped Block

in a paint tray, randomly dipping the sponge in the paint, then sponging through a purchased stencil. The three orange leaves in the center of the triangle were made by spraying paint through a stencil from a child's stencil set.

2 The purchased sunflower was stamped using bottle dabbers. The stamp was colored in with fabric markers.

3 Two different purchased stamps were used to create a border design for a purchased message block. The central image was painted with fabric markers.

4 A purchased stencil was used to add a delicate iris motif to an antique handkerchief. Lumiere paint was used to apply it with a stencil brush. The handkerchief was added by folding it over and fusing it in place.

5 Purchased alphabet stamps used bottle dabbers to stamp a message. The heart was added using basic no-sew appliqué. The small heart sequins were used to echo the central image.

6 This is an original-design stamp cut from a gum eraser. It was created by applying Lumiere paint to the stamp surface with a sponge brush, and stamped twice between repainting.

7 Spirals from purchased stamps, combined with heat-transferred motifs, were used to create the pattern on this piece. The small spirals were stamped by applying Lumiere paint to the stamp surface with a sponge brush. To make the large spirals, ink was applied using a bottle dabber.

Laces, Linens, and Appliqués Block

In addition to laces and linens, this block features a variety of appliqués, both pre- and custom-made. Review the list below, then reread "Laces, Linens, and Appliqués" in Chapter 4 for more ideas. (You will also find additional ideas on the other blocks for this quilt.) For pre-made fusible appliqués, follow the instructions provided; for nonfusible pre-made appliqués, apply with fabric glue or fusible adhesive. To make custom-made appliqués, bond a larger piece of paper-backed fusible adhesive to the back of the motif on the fabric; carefully cut the motif out, then remove the paper backing, and fuse in place. Any fabric can be cut apart to use for appliqué motifs, including paisleys, florals, animal prints, iron-on transfers, and pieces of worn or damaged linens, such as handkerchiefs and doilies.

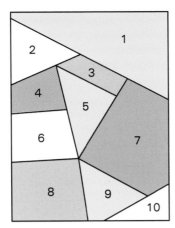

Fig. 7-7. Laces, Linens, and Appliqués Block

1 A heart-shaped piece of lace was used as an appliqué, with a premade embroidered appliqué glued on top. Iron-on transfers were used as decorative embellishments along the edge of the shapes.

2 A rooster motif cut from fabric and backed with fusible web to create a custom-made appliqué.

3 A row of purchased appliqués fills the patch.

4 An iron-on transfer of roses was used in this patch.

5 This patch is decorated with part of a linen handkerchief found at a flea market.

6 Purchased iron-on Ultrasuede appliqués were used in this patch.

7 This appliqué was made from a worn antique bureau runner. The numbers are purchased fabric appliqués.

8 These custom-made appliqués were created with image transfer. The background image was transferred to fabric and cut out as a rectangular appliqué. The cherubs were cut from fabric, then fused with paper-backed adhesive and cut out individually. See "Image Transfer" in Chapter 5 for more on this technique.

9 Purchased iron-on bead appliqué forms a fern frond shape. The top edge is lined with purchased iron-on Ultrasuede heart appliqués.

10 Purchased embroidered appliqués were used to embellish the raw edge.

Charms and Found Objects Block

Arrange the embellishments on your block. When you have created a satisfactory design, secure them with fabric glue, tie them on, or use any other method for securing them. The following is a guide to the embellishments on this block. Try them all, or experiment with one or two. Then explore other ways to embellish your block.

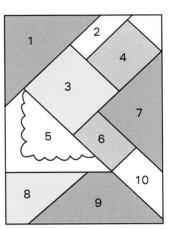

Fig. 7-8. Charms and Found Objects Block

1 Star sequins arranged as a decorative border between two pieces of fabric.

2 This is a fish from an earring.

3 Sun and moon charms on a piece of antique lace.

4 An image transfer made from acrylic gel, embellished with a brass cherub stamp and ribbon flowers. (See "Image Transfer" in Chapter 5 for information on image transfer.)

5 A brass stamp painted with Paint it Pretty paint, which is formulated specifically for metal and jewelry.

6 A scissors charm centered on a scrap of old fabric.

7 A small doily with a cameo in the center.

8 Antique velvet appliqué leaf with large beads arranged along the edge of two pieces of fabric.

9 Seashells arranged in a pattern.

10 Metal washers from the hardware store painted with Paint it Pretty paint.

Image Transfer Block

1 This image was created using heat transfer paper to turn a black-and-white photo into an antiqued print. (To create images like this, use heat-transfer paper and a photocopy of the photo. Simply cut the photocopy into any shape, then cut the transfer paper exactly the same. Place the transfer paper

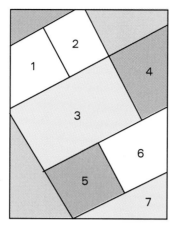

Fig. 7-9. Image Transfer Block

on top of the photocopy, then iron over it; the color is transferred to the copy, and in turn to the fabric.)

2 This block demonstrates a color photo gel transfer made from a color copy of a greeting card, using the face-down method.

3 This is a sun print of two feathers, showing wonderful details.

4 This is another image transfer of a black-and-white photo, using a liquid transfer medium in the face-up method on a colored fabric. Stamps were used to create a decorative border.

5 An image transfer of a black-and-white photo on a white fabric, using a liquid transfer medium in the face-down method, is outlined with buttons.

6 An illustration from an antique book was traced on a piece of tracing paper, then ironed onto a piece of fabric. (This technique eliminates mistakes on the fabric. Designs can be shaded or colored in using an iron-on transfer pen.)

7 Maple seeds were employed to create an overall pattern with sun printing. A purchased stencil sprayed with paint provides the leaf patterning.

PATTERNS

HOW TO USE THE FULL-SIZE PATTERNS

To make a master pattern, take a piece of tracing paper at least ½″ larger on each side than the block size. Fold it in half (fold 1), then fold it into quarters (fold 2). Open it up and number each quadrant for reference, as shown in Figure Pat-1. Match the quadrant numbers on the tracing paper to the numbers on the patterns. Align the center of the tracing paper with the center of the pattern quadrant, align the fold lines with the pattern lines. Place the tracing paper on top of the pattern in the book, and secure with drafting tape. Trace each quadrant, including the outside lines. Outline with a dark marker.

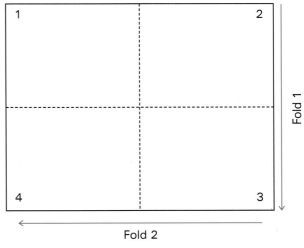

Fig. Pat-1.

Whimsical Cat Banner

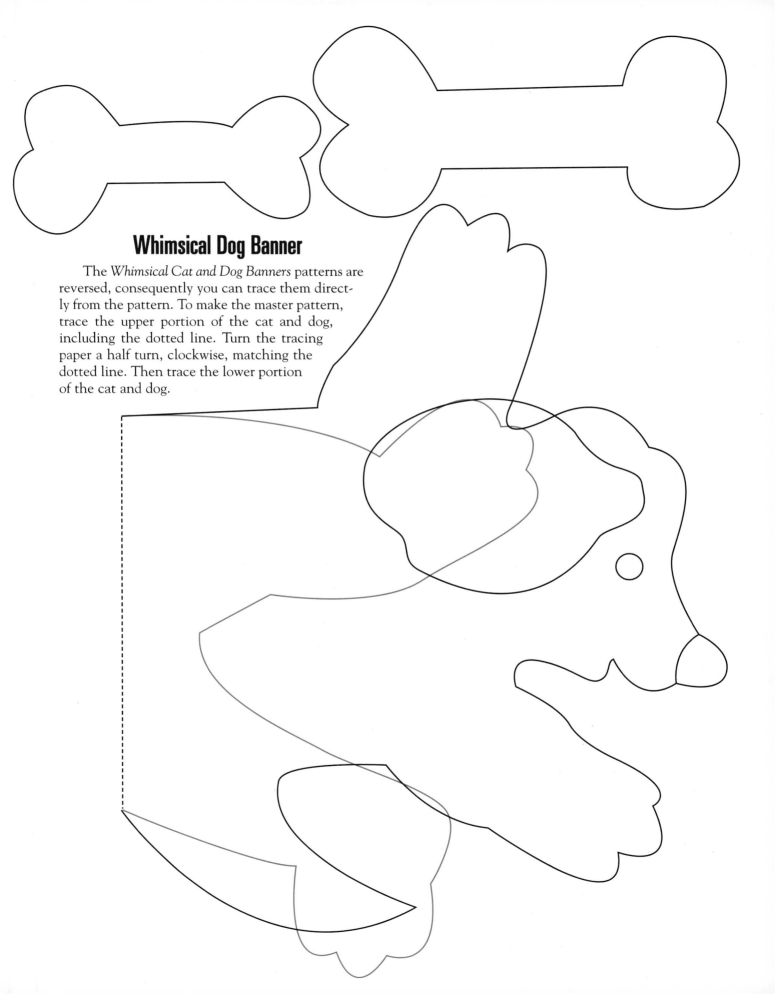

Whimsical Dog Banner

The *Whimsical Cat and Dog Banners* patterns are reversed, consequently you can trace them directly from the pattern. To make the master pattern, trace the upper portion of the cat and dog, including the dotted line. Turn the tracing paper a half turn, clockwise, matching the dotted line. Then trace the lower portion of the cat and dog.

Vase with Lilies

Art Nouveau Stained-Glass Window: Complete Pattern Block

To make the master pattern, trace the four quadrants, then trace the Small Window Pattern across the top and bottom of the quadrants as shown on the Complete Pattern Block. Then add a 2½″ border all around.

Art Nouveau Stained-Glass Window: Pattern Quadrant 1

Art Nouveau Stained-Glass Window: Pattern Quadrant 2

Art Nouveau Stained-Glass Window: Pattern Quadrant 3

Art Nouveau Stained-Glass Window: Small Window Pattern

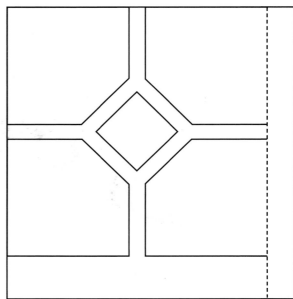

Pennsylvania Dutch Flowers:
Pattern Quadrant 2

Pennsylvania Dutch Flowers:
Pattern Quadrant 3

Pennsylvania Dutch Flowers:
Pattern Quadrant 1

Pennsylvania Dutch Flowers:
Pattern Quadrant 4

Pennsylvania Dutch Flowers: Pattern is reduced to 50%

Full-Blown Flowers Block: Pattern Quadrant 2

Full-Blown Flowers Block: Pattern Quadrant 3

Full-Blown Flowers Block: Pattern Quadrant 1

Full-Blown Flowers Block: Pattern Quadrant 4

Full-Blown Flowers Block: Pattern is reduced to 50%

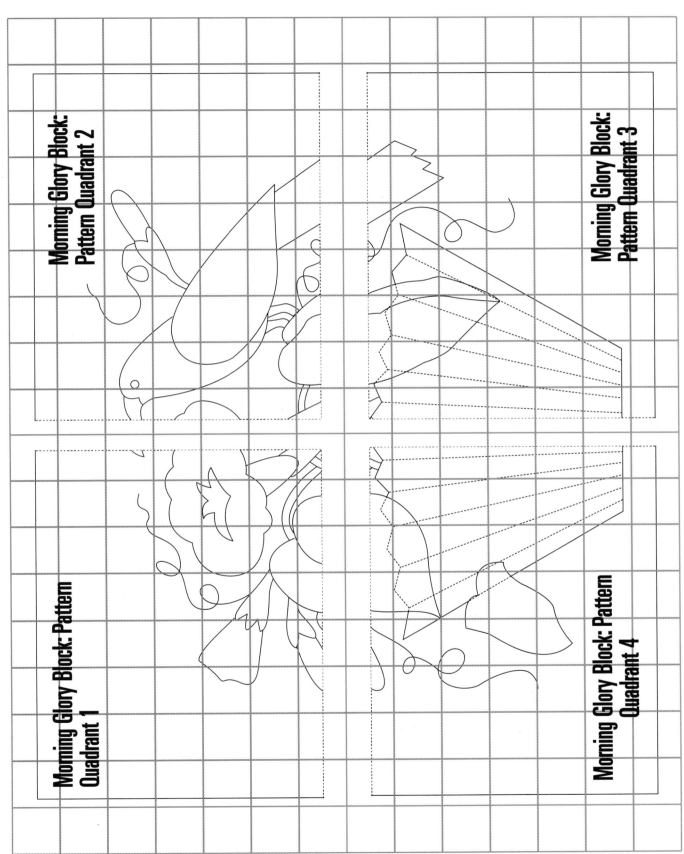

Morning Glory Block: Pattern is reduced to 50%

Woven Basket of Flowers
Block: Pattern Quadrant 2

Woven Basket of Flowers
Block: Pattern Quadrant 3

Woven Basket of Flowers
Block: Pattern Quadrant 1

Woven Basket of Flowers
Block: Pattern Quadrant 4

Woven Basket of Flowers Block: Pattern is reduced to 50%

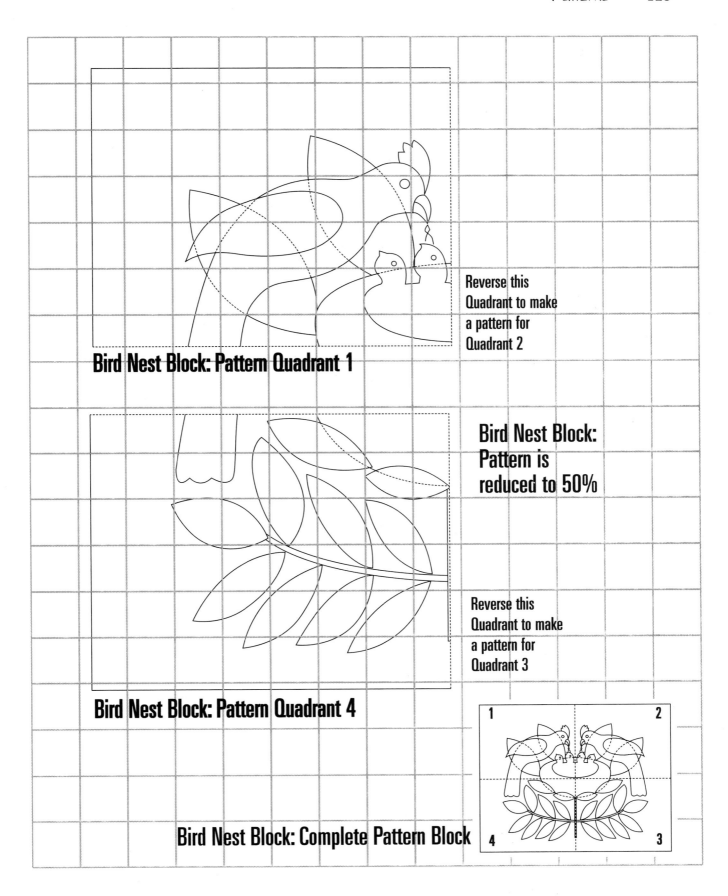

Bird Nest Block: Pattern Quadrant 1

Reverse this Quadrant to make a pattern for Quadrant 2

Bird Nest Block: Pattern is reduced to 50%

Reverse this Quadrant to make a pattern for Quadrant 3

Bird Nest Block: Pattern Quadrant 4

Bird Nest Block: Complete Pattern Block

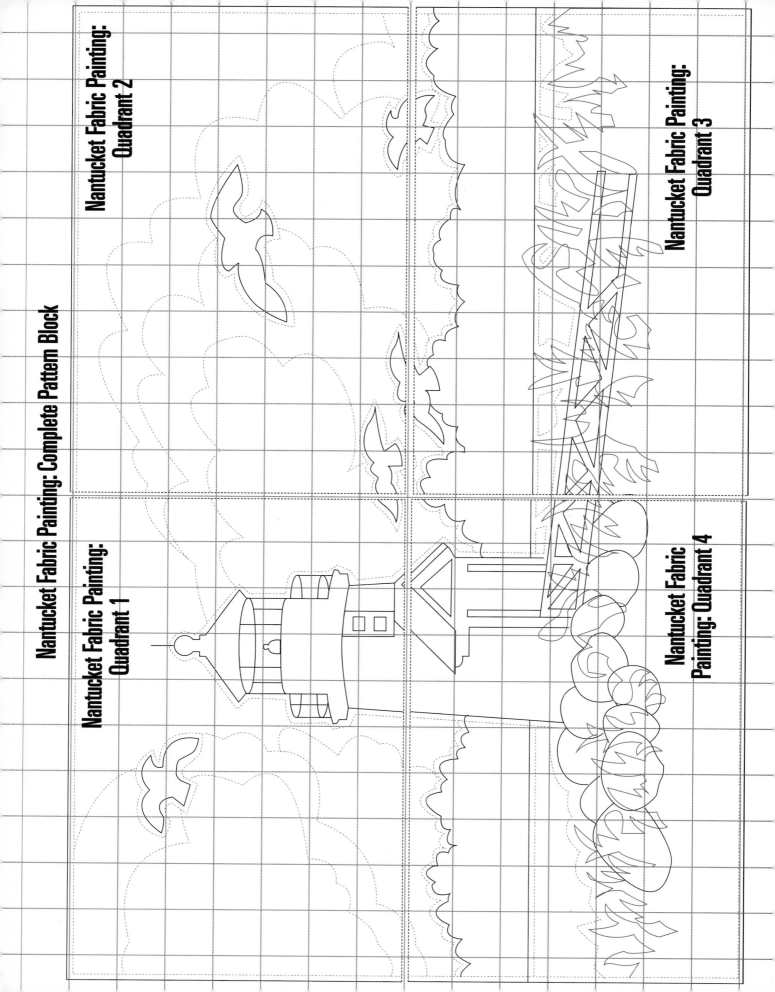

Nantucket Fabric Painting: Complete Pattern Block

Nantucket Fabric Painting:
Quadrant 1

Nantucket Fabric Painting:
Quadrant 2

Nantucket Fabric Painting:
Quadrant 3

Nantucket Fabric
Painting: Quadrant 4

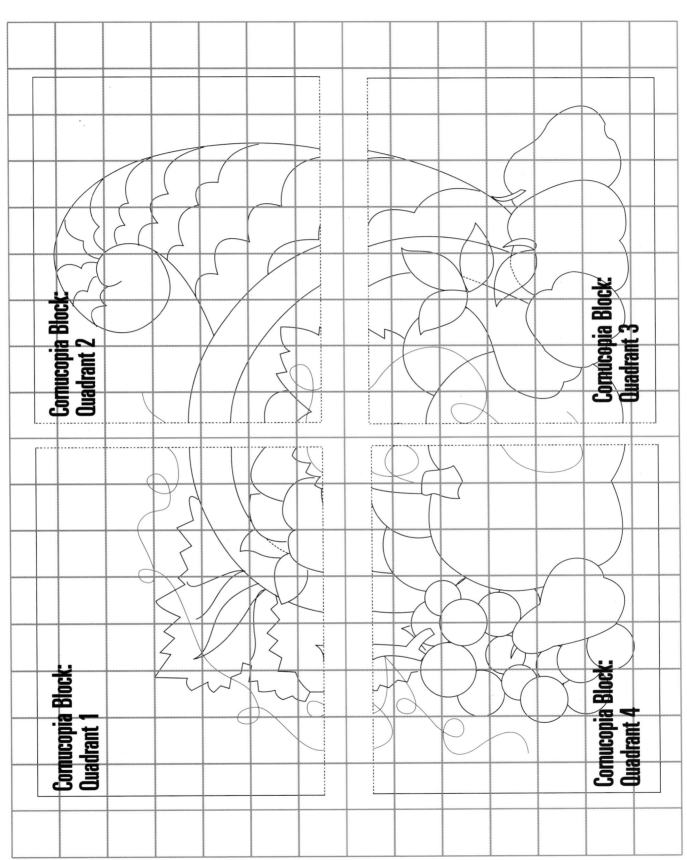

Cornucopia Block: Quadrant 2

Cornucopia Block: Quadrant 3

Cornucopia Block: Quadrant 1

Cornucopia Block: Quadrant 4

Cornucopia Block: Pattern is reduced to 50%

PRODUCTS LIST

Keep in mind that this list is only a starting point designed to familiarize you with the techniques and types of products you can use. By all means, experiment and explore other paints. Starter kits are available for many products and are a great way to become familiar with them.

Paint and Ink

Setacolor. The opaque colors can be used for most techniques on most fabrics; pearlescent and fluorescent paints are also available. The transparent colors are used for heliographic (sun) painting, spraying, and spattering.

Deka Permanent Fabric Paint. These are good, all-around versatile paints for all painting techniques; metallic, opaque, and fluorescent paints are also available.

Jones Tones Stretch Paint. This paint has an adhesive base so it can be used as a paint, glue, or dimensional paint, and can be used to paint, marble, spray, or spatter. It can also be used on Lycra, nylon, or hosiery.

FabricARTS "All Fabric" Paint. These transparent paints can be used on almost any fabric with almost any technique.

Lumiere and Neopaque Paints. These paints can be used for stamping, stencilling, painting, marbling, and painting on most fabrics as well as on wood, paper, and leather. The Lumiere paint is metallic and really contains metal. The Neopaque paint is very opaque and can be used effectively on dark fabrics.

Versatex Air Brush Ink. These feature intense color, and are good for spraying, painting, and marbling.

Createx Air Brush Colors. These are transparent colors that can be used on most fabrics as well as on other types of surfaces, including leather, plastic, and canvas.

Air-Tex Textile Air Brush Colors. These are opaque colors especially formulated to cover dark fabrics.

Stamp Dabber Fabric Ink, Fab Dab Fabric Ink. These are permanent fabric inks that come in a bottle with a dab-on top, thus eliminating the need for a stamp pad.

Image Transfer Products

Photo Transfer Mediums. A variety of products are available that can be used for image transfer, including By Jupiter! Pictures to Fabric Transfer Gel, Picture This Transfer Medium for Fabric, and Fabricraft Solutions.

Design Dye Paper. This is paper printed with color that can be used to transfer photocopies or other flat objects or designs to fabric.

Deka IronOn Transfer Paint. Use this paint to paint or stamp a design onto paper, allow it to dry, then iron the design onto fabric to transfer the image. You can also use it to make your own sheets of transfer paper.

Blueprints-Printables Treated Fabrics. These are prepared, blueprint-sensitized fabrics that are used to image transfer using the sun.

Sulky Iron-On Transfer Pens. These pens come in several colors, plus white, and can be used to draw or trace designs on paper. The images can then be transferred to fabric with an iron.

Markers and Pens

Setaskrib. These markers have transparent colors that can be used for drawing or coloring directly on fabric. They are available with fine or regular tips; refillable markers are also available.

FabricMate. These markers are available in many blendable colors and come with both brush and chisel tips.

Fashion Craft Fabric Markers. These have brush-style nibs that can be used to draw broad or fine lines.

Pigma Micron. Although these pens come in a limited number of colors, they have fine points that are ideal for detail work.

Identipen. These are double-ended markers with a fine tip at one end and an extra-fine point at the other. They write on nearly any surface, but come in a limited number of colors.

Printing and Stamping Materials

Flexible Printing Plate. Sometimes called Sure-Stamp, these make it easy to create your own stamps. Simply draw a design, cut it out with scissors, peel off the backing, and place the sticky side of the image on a block of wood or a piece of cardboard or foamcore. Then print or stamp with it.

E-Z Cut Printing Blocks. These have a slab of soft eraser material on them that you can carve to create images for printing.

PenScore Foam Stamps. These allow you to design your own foam-texture stamps and are reusable.

Spraying Supplies

Visions Air Painter. This is a simple-to-use tool, similar to an airbrush, that makes it easy to spray paint smoothly and evenly.

Spray Gun with Disposable Spray Unit. This is a handy item that lets you turn any jar of paint into an aerosol sprayer.

Breath Operated Sprayer. This air-sprays paint when you blow into a plastic tube.

Design Master Color Tool. These are ultrafine spray colors that are specifically formulated to use on fabrics. They are available in many colors and finishes.

RECOMMENDED READING

Bawden, Juliet. *The Art and Craft of Applique.* London: Grove Weidenfeld, 1991.

Brown, Pauline. *Applique.* London: Merehurst Press, 1989.

Cohen, Daniel and Paula, and Eden Gray. *Marbling on Fabric.* Leveland, Colorado: Interweave Press, 1990.

Dittman, Margaret. *The Fabric Lovers' Scrapbook.* Radnor, Pennsylvania: Chilton Book Co., 1988.

Fanning, Robbie and Tony. *The Complete Book of Machine Quilting.* 2nd Edition. Radnor, Pennsylvania: Chilton Book Company, 1994

Finnegan, Dianne. *Piece by Piece: The Complete Book of Quiltmaking.* New York: Prentice Hall Press, 1990.

Fons, Marianne, and Liz Porter. *Quilter's Complete Guide.* Birmingham, Alabama: Oxmoor House, Inc., 1993.

Fox, Sandi. *Wrapped in Glory: Figurative Quilts & Bedcovers 1700-1800.* New York: Thames and Hudson, Inc., 1990.

Honda, Isao. *The World of Origami.* Tokyo, Japan: Japan Publications Trading Co., 1965.

Kennedy, Jill, and Jane Varrall. *Everything You Ever Wanted To Know About Fabric Painting.* Cincinnati, Ohio: North Light Books, 1994.

Lawther, Gail. *The Complete Quilting Course.* Radnor, Pennsylvania: Chilton Book Co., 1992.

Milford, Susan. *Adventures in Art.* Charlotte, Vermont: Williamson Publishing Co., 1990.

Newman, Thelma R., Jay Harley Newman, and Lee Scott Newman. *Paper as Art and Craft.* New York: Crown Publishers, Inc., 1973.

Rich, Chris. *The Book of Paper Cutting: A Complete Guide to All the Techniques—With More Than 100 Project Ideas.* New York: Sterling Publishing Co., 1993.

Sienkiewicz, Elly. *Dimensional Applique: Baskets, Blooms, & Baltimore Borders.* Lafayette, California: C & T Publishing, 1993.

Simms, Ami. *How to Improve Your Quilting Stitch.* Flint, Michigan: Mallery Press, 1987

Tescher, Judy Mercer. *Dyeing & Over-Dyeing of Cotton Fabrics.* Paducah, Kentucky: American Quilter's Society, 1990.

SOURCES

Blueprints-Printables
1504 Industrial Way #7
Belmont, CA 94002
(800) 356-0445
Blueprint fabric and supplies for sun printing.

By Jupiter!
7146 North 58th Dr.
Glendale, AZ 85301
(800) 242-2574
Picture to Fabric Transfer Gel, brass charms.

Cache Junction: Seitec
2701 W. 1800 South
Logan, UT 84321
(800) 333-3279
Fabric dyes, iron-on transfers.

Churn Dash Designs
P.O. Box 60056, Dept DA
Seattle, WA 98160
Morning Glory products including cotton batting, notions.

Clearsnap, Inc.
P.O. Box 98
Anacortes, WA 98221
(800) 293-6634
Rubber stamps, PenScore Foam Stamps.

Clotilde, Inc.
2 Sew Smart Way B8031
Stevens Point, WI 54481
(800) 545-4002
Many fabric supplies, tools, fusibles and glues, Perfect Pleater.

Color Me Patterns
1617 Bear Creek Rd.
Kerrville, TX 78028
(800) 434-7288
Clothing patterns.

The Craft Shop
3716 E. Main St.
Mesa, AZ 85203
(800) 642-6762
Fusible Ultrasuede, lamé, iron-on appliqués.

Createx
14 Airport Park Road
East Granby, CT 06026
(203) 654-5505
Fabric dyes and paints, airbrush colors.

Dharma Trading Company
P.O. Box 150916
San Rafael, CA 94915
(800) 542-5227
Numerous fiber arts supplies, including fabric paints, dyes, marbling supplies, discharge paste color remover.

Diane Herbort Designs
3532 S. 16th St.
Arlington, VA 22204
Embellishments, photocopy transfer products. Send SASE for list.

Dick Blick
P.O. Box 1267
Galesburg, IL 61402
Art supplies, printing supplies, airbrushes, sprayers.

Domestications
P.O. Box 40
Hanover, PA
(717) 633-3313
Bed and table linens, curtains.

Earth Guild
33 Haywood St.
Asheville, NC 28801
(800) 327-8448
Fabric paints and dyes, supplies.

Hampton Art Stamps, Inc.
19 Industrial Blvd.
Medford, NY 11763
(800) 229-1019
Rubber stamps, Fab Dab Fabric Ink.

Ivy Imports, Inc.
12213 Distribution Way
Beltsville, MD 20705
(301) 595-0550
Fabric paints and dyes, textile supplies.

Jukebox
14128 Cameron Lane
Santa Ana, CA 92705
(714) 731-2563
Fabric markers, rubber stamps.

Maplewood Crafts
Humboldt Industrial Park
1 Maplewood Drive
Hazleton, PA 18201
(800) 899-0134
Heat-applied graphics, iron-on transfers.

Nancy's Notions, Ltd.
P.O. Box 683
Beaver Dam, WI 53916
(800) 833-0690
Many fabric supplies, notions and tools, fusibles and glues.

Pro Chemical & Dye, Inc.
P.O. Box 14
Somerset, MA 02726
(508) 676-3838
Fabric dyes, inks, and supplies.

Rubber Poet Rubber Stamps
Box 218F
Rockville, UT 84763
(801) 772-3441
Rubber stamps.

Rubber Stamp Zone
7771 Bridgeway #203
Sausalito, CA 94965
(800) 993-9119
Rubber stamps, Stamp Dabber Fabric Ink.

Sulfiati's Art Adventures
1024 Carlsbad St.
San Diego, CA 92114
(800) 377-7621
Fabric dyes.

Things Japanese
9805 NE 116th St.
Kirkland, WA 98034
(206) 821-2287
Silk dyes and paints, silk notions, instructions and kits.

INDEX